Business Development
for Women Lawyers
Second Edition

EDITED BY EVA TOWNSEND BILTON

Commissioning editor
Alex Davies

Managing director
Sian O'Neill

Business Development for Women Lawyers, Second Edition
is published by

Globe Law and Business Ltd
3 Mylor Close
Horsell
Woking
Surrey GU21 4DD
United Kingdom
Tel: +44 20 3745 4770
www.globelawandbusiness.com

Business Development for Women Lawyers, Second Edition

ISBN 978-1-83723-034-1
EPUB ISBN 978-1-83723-035-8
Adobe PDF ISBN 978-1-83723-036-5

© 2024 Globe Law and Business Ltd except where otherwise indicated.

The right of the contributors to be identified as authors of this work has been asserted by them in accordance with sections 77 and 78 of the Copyright, Designs and Patents Act 1988.

All rights reserved. No part of this publication may be reproduced in any material form (including photocopying, storing in any medium by electronic means or transmitting) without the written permission of the copyright owner, except in accordance with the provisions of the Copyright, Designs and Patents Act 1988 or under terms of a licence issued by the Copyright Licensing Agency Ltd (www.cla.co.uk). Applications for the copyright owner's written permission to reproduce any part of this publication should be addressed to the publisher.

DISCLAIMER
This publication is intended as a general guide only. The information and opinions which it contains are not intended to be a comprehensive study, or to provide legal advice, and should not be treated as a substitute for legal advice concerning particular situations. Legal advice should always be sought before taking any action based on the information provided. The publisher bears no responsibility for any errors or omissions contained herein.

Contents

Executive summary vii

About the authors xi

Foreword 1
By Rachel Brushfield, EnergiseLegal

**Chapter 1: Advancement and empowerment
of women lawyers – taking the credit** 3
By Natasha Innocenti, Empire Search Partners
    Making rain 3
    Now it's raining 4
    Myths 6
    Where credit is due 7

Chapter 2: The make-up of a rainmaker 9
By Pam Loch, Loch Associates Group
    Nature or nurture? 9
    Be client-centric 11
    Prepare to plan 12
    Be bold and be brave 13
    Create company collaboration 14
    Play the social strategy 15
    The feminine rainmaker 16

Chapter 3: Building reputation and relationships 19
By Susan Heaton-Wright, Superstar Communicator
    Why is professional reputation so important for lawyers? 19
    What are business relationships? 21
    Why do they differ to personal relationships? 22
    Building reputation 24

Why don't women do this?	25
Planning and effort	29

Chapter 4: Networking effectively and positively at events ... 33
By Joanna Gaudoin, Inside Out Image

The value of networking	33
Developing a strategy and plan	34
Preparing to go to events	36
Attending an event	38
Leaving people and moving on	42
After an event	43
In conclusion	44

Chapter 5: Female-friendly networking – the power of social media ... 47
By Belinda Lester, Lionshead Law

Facebook groups	50
LinkedIn	51
X (formerly known as Twitter)	52
Instagram/Threads	53

Chapter 6: Overcoming blocks around self-promotion ... 55
By Susan Heaton-Wright, Superstar Communicator

Remembering to acknowledge successes	60
The power of dual promotion	62
Building a library of case studies	62
How to structure your case studies or stories	63
Why it is important for women to take the credit and self-promote?	65

Chapter 7: Utilizing AI for strategic advantage in solo and small female-run firms ... 67
By Nika Kabiri, Kabiri Consulting

What is AI?	68
When to leverage AI	68
How to know what AI tools to use	70
Ethical considerations	72
Conclusion	73

Chapter 8: Using technology for business development 75
By Joanne Brook, Lionshead Law

    Introduction 75
    Small is beautiful 76
    Using tech to be a successful legal advisor 76
    Using tech to secure and develop your work 78
    Emotional intelligence 81
    Staying on board and riding the technology wave 82

Chapter 9: Culture, connection, and collegiality – creating a model that works for female lawyers 85
By Sarah Goulbourne, gunnercooke

    Experience – how being a woman shaped my career in the law 86
    Time for change – when and why I felt I could make a difference 86
    The early years – defining our mission and making it happen 87
    Celebrating success – how women at gunnercooke have
        made their mark 90
    This I have learned – passing on the wisdom 91

Chapter 10: What business development means to in-house lawyers – in conversation with top GCs 93
Interviews with Aniela Foster-Turner, Hannah Constantine, and Misha Patel

    Aniela Foster-Turner, ENODA 93
    Hannah Constantine, Smiths Group plc 95
    Misha Patel, JDG 97

Chapter 11: Mentoring and coaching 103
By Claire Rason, Client Talk

    What is the difference between mentoring and coaching? 103
    How coaching and mentoring are relevant to
        business development 105
    What makes it rain if not the rainmakers? 106
    Confidence and business development 107
    What is business development if not relationship
        management? 108
    What are the limiting beliefs that commonly show up
        around business development? 110
    Coaching and mentoring for results 111

**Chapter 12: Harnessing the true potential
of neurodivergent lawyers** 113
By Pam Loch, Loch Associates Group, and
Danielle Gleicher-Bates, neurodiversikey
    Navigating neurodiversity 113
    Evaluating the educational system 117
    Orientating the obstacles 119
    What else can become a stumbling block in the workplace? 120
    Making work, work 122
    Business development for neurodivergent lawyers 124
    Conclusion 125

About Globe Law and Business 129

Executive summary

As of 2023, women still only make up 37 percent of full equity partners in private practice law firms.[1] Business development – the people you know, your order book, and your ranking within an organization – is key to closing this gap. It might be a generalization to say that women do business development differently to men, but it tends to hold true. Crafting successful, authentic, out-of-the-box business development strategies in a largely male-dominated profession is a challenge for many women lawyers, who find that the status quo doesn't work for them.

This second edition of *Business Development for Women Lawyers* features contributions from a variety of women at the top of their field who've amassed a wealth of insight into how women can excel in the legal industry. Our contributors look at the skills and techniques, experiences, and talents that female lawyers use to develop their practices and grow their order books, acting as both inspiration and motivation to readers. From frank discussions about when to use AI to guidance on navigating the sometimes frightening world of networking events, readers will come away with a clear understanding of how to get ahead in the legal world.

Client development is table stakes for women lawyers aspiring to "rainmaker" status at their firm. The crucial next step for women attorneys is ensuring they receive their due credit for those clients and matters they developed. In our opening chapter, Natasha Innocenti explores the essential traits of women rainmakers who have successfully navigated the gender biases and occasionally draconian complexities of law firm compensation systems. Emphasized skills include creative networking, internal marketing, practiced confidence, and even generative AI know-how. Natasha confronts prevailing myths surrounding various credit origination systems and how women can successfully navigate within them.

The traditional networker will attend conferences, write insightful blogs, arrange client lunches and dinners, and show up at the networking platforms – but this list of business tactics doesn't create the rainmaker alone. So what does create that status? What sets them apart from another partner? What traits do these individuals hold, and is it possible to nurture and train up your team to create an army of rainmakers? Pam Loch answers these questions in chapter two, in a deep dive into what makes an effective rainmaker.

Building your professional reputation and relationships within your firm, with clients, and within the industry as a whole is essential for career and business success. In chapter three, Susan Heaton-Wright discusses why it's important to build a positive reputation and relationships with others, what might be stopping you from doing so, and some ideas, tips, and activities to help build up your reputation and your network.

Attending networking events can feel daunting for many. Learning the key skills to network at events effectively and positively, together with practicing those skills, will lead to increased confidence and positive outcomes at events and afterwards. Joanna Gaudoin's chapter looks at the need for and benefit to networking, which goes far beyond what people often think, to help individuals navigate the working world and progress their careers. The chapter discusses how to develop a networking strategy and plan before walking through the key skills you need to navigate networking events well, from the moment you arrive until you leave, as well as what to do afterwards. Events themselves are simply an initial way to meet people and begin new professional relationships. But nowadays, nurturing your online network is as important as any in-person connections you make.

In chapter five, Belinda Lester talks about the power of social media, the school gate, and female friendships. She explores how the COVID-19 pandemic and subsequent lockdown, as well as the trend that this led to working from home, has enabled women to leverage their networking power and, in some ways, now puts men at a distinct disadvantage. Belinda discusses, in particular, the power of Facebook and how it differs from LinkedIn, and how both these platforms as well as other social media can be best used to complement in-person networking and maximize their benefit. Belinda explains how she has utilized her online network as well as her offline one to generate tens of thousands of pounds worth of business, as well as to attract lawyers to her firm.

A key characteristic of any successful person is that they take credit for their contribution – they have control over their career and ensure others know their successes. The challenge for many women is that culturally they are brought up not to self-promote, which negatively impacts their career prospects. In chapter six, Susan Heaton-Wright talks about why it's important to take credit for your contributions and ownership for your career successes, as well as why many women might find this a challenge. Self-promotion and owning your success not only has an important impact on your mindset but can help you forge positive connections with others and build a strong reputation both within and outside of your firm.

One area for discussion stands out above the rest when considering how the legal profession is evolving – artificial intelligence (AI). In most cases, surviving and thriving as a practice means being tech-forward. Small and solo-run firms often don't have the resources to hire staff when support is needed, so software for scheduling, accounting, legal research, and practice management may be essential. It's not surprising, then, that many female lawyers are wondering how AI might give them an advantage in their small and solo-run practices. AI can reduce time spent on tedious tasks while tremendously improving the quality of information-gathering and analysis. Most importantly, AI can improve decision-making by making it better informed and less biased. Because of these obvious benefits, many firms are leveraging AI without much hesitation. But AI is a tool, not a cure-all, and like all tools, it is most useful when it solves problems it is suited to solve. In chapter seven, Nika Kabiri discusses how and when is best to adopt AI into your practice.

Legal optimizers have already adopted tech tools to crunch data and actively use it to identify clients and improve chances of engagement by exploring metrics of previous deals, outcomes, advice, and costs. Many larger firms also already use the advantage of AI tools to achieve their goals with less effort and more efficiency. In chapter eight, Joanne Brook considers that, as we move from the phase of "early adoption" of AI for legal practice, this is the time for the majority to review the initial success of its use in legal practice and the advantages that can be gained in using new technology.

While the traditional law firm model promises lawyers a prestigious career path and generous financial compensation, to progress to the top often means sacrificing a healthy work–life balance, which disproportionately impacts female legal professionals. In chapter nine, Sarah Goulbourne, co-founder of gunnercooke, explains how her belief that legal services could be delivered differently has created a new model that is challenging this gender imbalance. Sarah shares her experience of creating a law firm that prioritizes a healthy work–life balance and puts culture at its center.

Good leadership is vital to creating a healthy culture that nurtures female talent, and in chapter ten, we speak to three GCs about what they do in their day-to-day lives to develop their own business and support the women around them. Aniela Foster-Turner, Hannah Constantine, and Misha Patel discuss putting client relations first, leading by example, and the importance of getting an early start to the day.

As touched on by our interviewees in chapter ten, mentoring and coaching have a big role to play in helping to enhance the business development skills of female lawyers. In chapter 11, Claire Rason sets out the differences between mentoring and coaching and shows how both can be harnessed. Exploring how confidence and other limiting beliefs can get in the way of winning work and doing business development, she provides an account of how individuals can use mentoring and coaching to leverage their strengths to excel.

The final chapter of the book looks at the everyday obstacles that women juggle in the legal workplace and considers the effect that such obstacles have on neurodivergent women lawyers. Pam Loch and Danielle Gleicher-Bates call for a future where neurodivergent talent is recognized, welcomed, and accepted, and discuss the steps that a firm needs to take to make work, work.

References
1   www.sra.org.uk/2023-firm-diversity-data-pay-gaps

About the authors

Joanne Brook is a legal technologist and provides advice to innovators across the creative sectors, from software developers to theatre producers and from AI developers to NFT artists. She focuses on helping clients achieve commercial solutions to previously not considered legal issues that arise from developing and using their technology and critically, in protecting and licensing their intellectual property rights to ensure business expansion and growth in a fast-paced market. Prior to becoming a legal consultant, she was a partner at a West End law firm and a boutique City law firm before that. She describes her view on the digital revolution and adoption of technology as like sitting in the jump seat with a super-sonic test pilot and hearing the engines roar or calmly evacuating the plane whilst wearing a parachute and hi-vis, carrying a laptop and inflating a lifeboat. In all that, she feels privileged to continue to advise smarter and more creative people than herself on a daily basis. Joanne is an intellectual property professional expert for Lexis Nexis and an author of IP and data management precedents for various professional publications. She regularly contributes legal insight to the legal press and lectures on technology and new law.

Rachel Brushfield is "The Talent Liberator", a career strategist, and coach who helps women lawyers to achieve uplifting breakthroughs at major career crossroads. Portfolio careers, thought leadership, and personal branding are specialisms. Rachel is founder of EnergiseLegal, established in 1986. Her chapters for Globe Law and Business include "Work's not working – portfolio careers" (*Career Development For Women Lawyers*), "Helping women lawyers overcome their blocks about marketing" *(Business Development For Women Lawyers)*, "The shifting sands of talent management" (*The Rise of Specialist Career Paths in Law Firms*), "Adapting business models to ride the millennial wave" (*Future Law Firm Business Models*), and "Essential skills for the changing legal market" (*The Talent Management Toolkit For Law Firms*). Books include T*alent Management – A Hands-on Guide, Professional Development for Lawyers*, and *Smarter Legal Marketing and Career Management for*

Lawyers for the Law Society. Rachel has also written many articles for *Managing Partner* and The Law Society's *Managing for Success* and *Inside Out* magazines.

Hannah Constantine is a lawyer with wide corporate, M&A, and commercial experience. She is currently general counsel for corporate and M&A at Smiths Group plc, a FTSE 100 engineering group, which has offered her valuable opportunities to develop in a range of roles – from generalist commercial positions in Europe and Asia, to legal operations, to global corporate advisory and M&A. Hannah was highly commended in the "General Counsel of the Year" category at the Women & Diversity in Law Awards 2024. She established and chairs the Smiths Group Foundation, launched in 2023 with an initial commitment of £10 million to make impactful grants improving STEM skills access, safety, connectedness, and sustainability in Smiths Group's communities around the world. Prior to joining Smiths Group, Hannah spent eight formative years at Freshfields Bruckhaus Deringer.

Aniela Foster-Turner is a senior executive with over two decades of international legal and compliance experience in the energy sector. Aniela is the general counsel for Enoda, a tech company in the energy sector. She has worked in private equity for a couple of years, developing battery storage projects in four different jurisdictions. Prior to that, she held previous leadership roles with Siemens and Siemens Gamesa, where she broke ground as the company's first woman general counsel in Europe and worked on the development of over seven GW of wind farm projects. She is widely recognized as one of the foremost lawyers in highly complex, high-profile transactions within the renewable industry. Aniela was shortlisted for "Woman of the Year" at the Law Society Excellence Awards 2019 and the "Innovative Leader" and "In-House Leader" of the Year awards at Women, Influence & Power 2021 and 2022. She is an ambassador of POWERful Women, a mentor in the legal community, and a non-executive director on the board of trustees of the Women in Engineering Society earlier in 2023.

Aniela has two legal degrees from the University of Bucharest and City University of London, as well as studying European Law at King's College, and is a Saïd Oxford Business School alumna. She uses her broad knowledge, heritage, and experience to promote and support various diversity and inclusion initiatives while championing change in the legal profession.

Joanna Gaudoin, Inside Out Image, helps lawyers to excel at professional relationships to navigate workplace challenges, be the best they can be at work, and fulfil their potential – ultimately to progress their careers and improve the performance of their firm. Joanna works with individuals, firms via group sessions, and speaks at events to help lawyers move forward from where they are, including being promoted, dealing with the new aspects of a role following a promotion, handling challenging relationships, developing client and prospect relationships, managing others, and building their profile and network in the market. Fundamentally, her work helps people consider how they are engaging with others at work and improve their communication to relate to others in different work scenarios effectively and positively to build better professional relationships and achieve their objectives. She is the author of *Getting On: Making work work*, and a highly experienced trainer and speaker.

Danielle Gleicher-Bates is an award-winning neurodiversity advocate passionate about neuroinclusion in the legal sector and justice system. As a late-diagnosed, multiple-neurodivergent woman, she uses her lived experience to challenge perceptions of neurodivergence. Danielle is the co-founding chair of neurodiversikey® and an aspiring barrister, having been awarded scholarships by the Honourable Society of the Inner Temple and City Law School to pursue the Bar Vocational Studies course.

As the co-founder of gunnercooke, **Sarah Goulbourne** is passionate about challenging, improving, and evolving the way in which legal services are delivered to businesses. Sarah is also hugely passionate about creating a business model that gives lawyers the opportunity to use the best of their legal abilities, in a way that motivates them. She is adamant that people should be able to practice law without sacrificing their personal life, something that many lawyers find difficult in the more traditional environments. Sarah has over 20 years' experience practicing commercial law in a range of organizations, including FTSE 250 companies, private entrepreneurial businesses, and the public sector. She has held numerous executive and non-executive board positions, working in the leisure, media, financial, and health sectors. She is an experienced non-executive director and has a detailed knowledge of merger and acquisitions and governance requirements in listed companies.

About the authors

Susan Heaton-Wright is a multi-award-winning businesswoman, international keynote speaker, former prize-winning opera singer, author, podcaster, and the founder of Superstar Communicator, empowering emerging leaders to communicate with impact, confidence, clarity, and credibility in all business conversations. These include delivering speeches, presenting ideas and opinions, pitching for investment, public speaking, and being effective in meetings. Her company works with many pharmaceutical multinational companies and professional services firms. She has worked with attendees from more than 130 countries worldwide. Susan is a launch leader for EMEA leadership programs for HBA. In 2020, she was named as one of the top 100 Influential Female Entrepreneurs in the UK. Susan visits Athens annually to support the Love Without Borders charity, which supports refugees. She also fundraises for the Alzheimer's Society and the Isabel Hospice in Hertfordshire.

Natasha Innocenti is a partner at Empire Search. She has been recruiting partners and groups in California at the highest levels since 1997. Natasha started her legal search career at Heidrick & Struggles. She spent almost 15 years at Major, Lindsey & Africa, as a partner and head of the partner practice in the Bay Area for eight years. In 2017, she joined Macrae, where she and her team executed searches for prestigious law firms looking to open and expand in Northern California. Natasha has been named one of the 100 Leading Legal Consultants and Strategists by Law Dragon in each year since 2018. She has been writing and speaking on diversity and inclusion in the law for over 20 years. Natasha has served on the Board of the Law Foundation of Silicon Valley since 2013. She graduated from Mills College and earned her MA in Philosophy from the University of London in 1995.

Nika Kabiri is a decision scientist who has spent 20+ years studying decision-making in a variety of contexts, from relationships to politics to business. She is founder and principal at *Kabiri Consulting*, where she helps businesses improve their decision-making with AI. Nika's work on decision-making has been featured in Fast Company and Yahoo!, and she was recognized as a top decision coach in *LA Weekly*. She has been quoted in the *Wall Street Journal*, *Time*, *The Washington Post* and Gizmodo and has contributed to media sources like *The Hill*, *Huffington Post*, and Inside Sources. She is also co-author of the bestselling book *Money Off the Table: Decision Science and the Secret to Smarter Investing*. Nika has worked with clients like Amazon, Google, and Microsoft, as well as companies in the legal tech space. She is also a former University of Washington faculty member. Nika earned her PhD from the University of Washington and her JD from the University of Texas.

Pam Loch is a dual qualified solicitor who set up Loch Associates Group in 2007 to respond to the need for bespoke people solutions. Today, Loch Associates Group is a legal, HR, and training and wellbeing organization with a purpose of creating responsible, performing, and progressive businesses. As well as being the managing director, Pam has also been a specialist, award-winning employment law solicitor for over 20 years, writing thought-leading articles and book chapters, as well as being a seasoned commentator on television and radio. Pam has been ranked, for the last 13 years, as a Leading Solicitor in Employment Law in the *Legal 500* and *Chambers and Partners* legal guides, with Loch Law being ranked as a leading firm too. Her passion for finding solutions to help businesses manage and look after their people is reflected in the development and success of the businesses across the group.

Belinda Lester, the managing director and founder of Lionshead Law, is an employment lawyer with 25 years' experience in the field. Acting for both employers and employees, her first degree in psychology has been invaluable both in relation to her work in dispute resolution and in relation to business development. She started her firm in 2013 and has grown the consultancy-based practice from solely offering employment law services to one that now includes commercial, immigration, and private client work. As a working mother of two, she had to find creative ways to network and finds utilizing social media to build her brand invaluable.

Misha Patel is a seasoned English law-qualified corporate/commercial lawyer and the general counsel at JDG. She began her career at Clifford Chance, where she trained and excelled as a senior associate. She then spent 12 years at KPMG UK as its associate general counsel and legal director, specialising in M&A transactions, regulatory compliance, and corporate/commercial matters. Misha's extensive experience includes Board-level and international mandates, navigating complex legal, risk, and strategic challenges. Known for her leadership and pragmatic guidance, she adeptly manages tech, operational, and compliance issues. A recognised speaker at various conferences and roundtables, Misha's insights have earned her recognition as a "Rising

Star" by Financial News, the *Sunday Times*, and Management Today, highlighting her influence and impact in the legal and financial sectors.

Misha holds a law degree from the University of London and a master's in law from the University of Warwick. Her educational background, combined with her extensive professional experience, positions her as a formidable legal leader.

Claire Rason is an accredited coach (Senior Practitioner Level with the EMCC). She is the founder of coaching consultancy Client Talk. A former practicing solicitor, she has worked in, or alongside, professional services firms for over 20 years. Claire is passionate about bringing the power of active listening and diverse thinking to professional services firms. She is particularly passionate about gender parity at partnership level and has researched why women don't make it to the top (Class of 2002: Women in Law).

Foreword

Over 20 years' focus on women lawyers, numerous events for women's networks, including the American Women Lawyers in London (AWLL), the Association of Women Solicitors, London, Surrey, and Manchester groups and the Women Lawyers Division of the Law Society and law firms, has consistently reinforced one thing to me about women lawyers and business development.

Many women lawyers find business development (BD) uncomfortable, pushy, and boastful and therefore procrastinate and/or avoid it. It brings out their imposter syndrome – "Who am I to think that...".

Turning BD on its head to what motivates women and reframing it to helping people, educating and building relationships etc. works. "Blowing your own trumpet" – my most popular event topic for women lawyers, and indeed women in general – is deeply uncomfortable for many women. This is, however, gradually shifting with Generation Z more comfortable with promoting themselves than the Baby Boomers and Generation X have been.

Exploring limiting beliefs about business development and transforming them is vital. I remember probing with one coaching client their belief about "I hate networking". This led to useful insights to help them to reframe it. Their belief turned into, "I like chatting to people. And I enjoy connecting people with useful resources."

Women lawyers may have less time to do business development because they are (often) working parents and do a disproportionate amount of household management, so cannot do breakfast networking, or business dinners in the evening.

COVID-19 and working from home changed the playing field for women lawyers and business development. It opened up a whole new world of opportunity with online networking.

Framing BD in women lawyers' minds so that it is appealing, not repellent, is vital, and I encourage women lawyers to do one aspect of business development that they enjoy and are good at, really well, and not to worry about all the different elements. In other words, play to their strengths and make it a regular habit.

Many a time, I have asked the D+I manager at a law firm if they think women and men are different. The answer that they express is, "They are the same".

I do not agree. How can men and women be the same? I believe we need to stop tip-toing around D&I political correctness, because it is not helping women lawyers to be themselves and do business development *their* way and excel.

This multi-author book contains a wealth of different perspectives and insights. The topics explored include AI, networking, empowerment, mentoring and coaching, neurodiversity, overcoming blocks, rainmakers, social media, and technology.

The 12 chapters and 14 contributors are diverse, giving a wealth of perspectives from deep knowledge and experience. They are lawyers, founders of their own law firms, recruiters, and GCs working in-house. They all have something to say. I'd encourage you to jot down key insights that "speak to you" as you read what they have to say and set five SMART actions with deadlines.

If nothing else, one simple action that you can take from reading this book is to connect with the authors and the Globe Law and Business team on LinkedIn, and build your online network. You never know what opportunities, collaborations, new clients, introducers, or jobs could result, now or in the future. Business development, after all, is multifaceted and a combination of focus, strategy, habit, follow up, planning, and happenstance.

Rachel Brushfield
The Talent Liberator

Chapter 1:
Advancement and empowerment of women lawyers – taking the credit

By Natasha Innocenti, partner, Empire Search Partners

Making rain

Solving problems, networking, and building relationships are all skills many women lawyers possess. Each of these qualities aligns seamlessly with sales and business development. This is what we are good at. But the key to autonomy in a career as a law firm partner is to have your own clients. With clients comes opportunity, growth, compensation, and even power.

What qualities does a law firm rainmaker possess? First and foremost, they are great lawyers. Excellence in legal acumen is the ticket to entry. Rainmakers are good listeners, retaining the information from prospective clients about what they expect, want, and need. Rainmakers are creative, not only around deal or litigation strategy, but also when it comes to establishing and nurturing relationships. It isn't enough to attend any and all networking events. Better to strategically select such events for the kind of network you intend to build. Try to find out who will be there in advance. If you know someone who is attending, see if you can go together. Ask that person to introduce you to two others at the event you want to know. Follow up afterward with thoughtful responses and a suggestion of another way to get time together.

One woman rainmaker I know does walking meetings with women clients. They get out of the office, get some exercise, and build a bond that is more personal. Another woman law firm partner I know will selectively invite prospective women clients to get a pedicure together. Be creative in a way that is consistent with your style, and that won't reinforce gender stereotypes (your male general counsel client or someone you don't know well might be less enthusiastic about getting your nails done together and view it as a frivolous suggestion).

Rainmakers are confident enough to ask for the business, or the referral. They may not have been born that way, but have developed the confidence and skill through practice, being mentored, watching others, hiring coaches, reading books, and even role playing. Sadly, many have coupled this confidence with the knowledge that, for women, confidence needs to be calibrated appropriately. We live with a double standard in which men are tough and women are shrill, men confident and women "break too much glass". (An ironic metaphor to be sure, but on point nonetheless.) Many women rainmakers have learned to navigate, even utilize, the reality of the double standard instead of simply chafing under it. The more women rainmakers succeed, the less time we will have to live with that double standard.

Rainmakers know how to negotiate, and don't stop striving to improve their negotiating skills. I know many women lawyers who continue their education proactively, attending conferences and "boot camps" on marketing and negotiation, reading books on how to ask for what they want and not settle for no. Their confidence and creativity may border on the audacious, in a good way. I know a woman law firm partner who built a strong practice in the gaming space – one notoriously hard for women to break into. She did so in part by designing a business card depicting her as an animated superhero, with superpowers to protect her clients' intellectual property, establish their brand, you get the idea. The gaming executives loved it and it became a powerful ice breaker and reputation builder.

Keep in mind that in our modern age of generative artificial intelligence, creative business development content – like the superhero business card example above – can be had by even those attorneys devoid of design chops. There are a host of AI tools on the market that can generate an inventive business card image, pitch deck, data visualization, or other business development asset with just a single-sentence prompt. Much of the buzz around AI in the legal industry is concentrated on automating routine tasks and capturing process efficiencies (which, incidentally, should free up more time for business development!). However, AI's role as your personal creative assistant should not be overlooked, especially if one intends to stay ahead of the curve of the competition.

Now it's raining

So you've built up a client base, and a targeted network capable of giving you or referring you new business. The work isn't over to fully build your practice, but you are bringing in your own client work. You've ensured that the work you are doing is at the appropriate level for your firm; your rate isn't much too high for matters you are handling; you can leverage associates to help support the practice to make it more profitable; and your practice is one that your partners can cross-sell to their client base. You've done the internal marketing to make sure your partners understand what you do, and when it is appropriate to bring you in as a subject matter expert for your practice area. You are landing some of those cross-sold opportunities and taking the lead on the work for your partners' clients. You also have confidence that your practice area is important to your firm and you can expect resources and management time to be devoted, in part, to helping you and your team expand the practice.

Assuming most of the above is true, you are in a strong position within your firm and you have established yourself, even if you are still young and in build mode. But how do you know if you are getting appropriate credit within your firm's compensation system relative to your contribution? How does your firm's compensation system really work? Do you know? What have you been told? Does that align with what you have seen and experienced?

In some firms, it is challenging to know how the compensation system really works. In others, it is theoretically possible to know, but no one will tell you and the culture is one of "we don't ask". In others, your and everyone else's financial metrics, including compensation, are available for all to see. The financial metrics may even be pushed to the partnership proactively. Lock step systems are rare these days, but lock step firms and firms that modified their lock step systems retain transparency and don't rely as much on originations.

Most firms track origination credit, but it is important to know if they track the first touch for that client, or the origination of a particular matter. The latter system tends to value specialists and leads to more cross-selling within the firm. Some firms have a defined credit of 100 percent total, which can be split among the partners who pitched for the work. Some firms allocate 200 percent total credit. The important thing is that your system values everyone who helped land the matter. Credit systems that do not value up-and-coming partners, specialists, and/or lateral partners will undermine a firm's growth strategy and diversity programs.

In most compensation systems it is possible to be underpaid relative to your revenue and overall value. In fact, it is all too common to see a gender gap in law firm partner compensation, even for women with strong origination numbers. But, when women partners are undercompensated, it is most often because they are not given the credit they deserve for landing new matters.

For example, firms are often putting pitch teams together for large matters where more than one firm is competing for the work. Enlightened firms are ensuring that the team reflects diversity. Many clients now demand diverse teams. However, having a diverse pitch team and having a diverse team handling the matter are two different things. Sometimes one team brings the matter in, but only a subset of that team gets credit for doing so and then takes on leading the matter. Guess who? Often the grey-haired, white men who hold the relationship with the client, despite needing you and your expertise to win a particular matter.

Myths
Compensation systems range from a founding partner in a room by himself with a pencil and a legal pad (and it is almost always a "him") to a highly systematized process involving "brag" memos, many one-on-one interviews with partners, seemingly endless committee meetings, and a defined appeals process. Regardless of how much process is involved in how your firm establishes compensation, it is up to you to understand what really goes on behind the compensation committee doors, and how much your hard work bringing in client matters is valued. But before I address best practices for acquiring this understanding, I think it's important that I dispel a few popular myths about law firm compensation systems.

Here are some commonly held beliefs about law firm compensation that are not necessarily true:
- "Blind" or "Black Box" compensation systems, in which partners have little to no visibility into what their partners earn, are used to allow for unfair compensation allocations;
- Pure – or even mostly – formula-driven compensation systems encourage internal competition; and
- Firms that do not track origination credit in any formal way are more collaborative.

Of course, there are examples of each of the above systems that fit the myth. But for every firm that sustains the cliché, there are many others that disprove it. Some firms enhance collaboration by keeping partner compensation confidential. Over the past 28 years I've worked with firms that used their blind compensation system in an utterly fair and even-handed way, ensuring that the compensation process is relatively painless and takes much less management time. On the other hand, I've seen some firms "hide" an incredibly wide delta between the lowest paid and the highest paid partners with their black box comp system.

Pure formula systems can eliminate bias. In fact, when one is evaluated entirely on the merits – in this case, revenue origination and proliferation – many disputes are eliminated. Unfortunately, such a system under-rewards firm citizenship and non-monetary contributions, and "soft" contributions may be fewer from billing partners in a firm with a formula-based comp system. On the other hand, some firms with complete transparency, and the resulting scuffles and competition around compensation, can sometimes avoid unexamined bias – perceived or real. Lawyers can be quick to dismiss formula-based compensation systems, citing cultural challenges resulting from a true meritocracy. However, unexamined bias has fewer places to hide in such a system (hoarding clients or credit can certainly still occur, but that is more in the straight out-and-out bias category).

While firms that consider themselves to have transcended the need to track origination credit do often have collaborative cultures, this is not always the case. For example, I've worked closely with a firm that does not track origination credit as a matter of firm policy. Although such a system does nurture teambuilding and sharing of client work, in moments of candor, members of the compensation committee have indicated to me that they all "sort of know who really brings in the work". Many such firms have a more anecdotal way of allocating value. Members of the compensation committee have a higher bar to meet in such firms, since all law firms are businesses evaluated on their profitability as well as their quality. Such a system can encourage internal competition so the "right people" know who is making the rain.

Where credit is due

Whether your firm invites discussion about compensation or not, there is a way to talk about it, and learn about it, which mitigates risk and maximizes opportunity.

I encourage laterals and newly elected partners to seize their transition as an opportunity to learn all they can about their firm's system of allocating credit and setting compensation. When being considered for partner election, or as a potential lateral partner, you have a chance to sit down with the key decision-makers about compensation, and not only ask questions, but begin a conversation that will continue as long as you are a partner with that firm. This discussion can also occur at your annual compensation review process.

Ask how your firm values origination credit. How does that value stack up against other factors when determining compensation? What culture is the firm trying to uphold with the compensation system they have in place? Who are the key decision-makers when it comes to compensation? What do they care about?

Fortune 500 and other large companies are increasingly looking for diverse pitch teams. But now they are looking for more than that. Enlightened and sophisticated general counsel expect to see diversity in the pitch meeting, but they now expect to see diversity in the team actually handling their matters. More than once, a woman partner has told me she was in the pitch meeting, but then was not given any opportunity to handle the legal work resulting from that meeting. If you helped bring in such a matter, make sure you are getting credit for it. And once you have ensured you have been given credit, as appropriate, then turn and work to develop the women more junior to you. Help them understand how things really work in your firm. Give them pointers on how to negotiate compensation, credit, and value.

Help to ensure that the next generation experiences a little less bias, a little more fairness, and help give credit where credit is due.

Chapter 2:
The make-up of a rainmaker

By Pam Loch, founder, Loch Associates Group

A rainmaker. Sometimes considered the mythical creature of business development. The ability of an individual to have the magical touch to not just bring in revenue but to attract and retain clients with effortless ease. Originating in the legal profession, the term rainmaker has gained traction in other industries, from investment banking to political campaigning, applying to an individual's ability to "turn the tide" or generate sustained business success.

The traditional networker will attend conferences, write insightful blogs, arrange client lunches and dinners, and show-up at the networking platforms – but this list of business tactics doesn't create the rainmaker alone.

So, what creates that status? What sets them apart from another partner? What traits do these individuals hold, and is it possible to nurture and train up your team to create an army of rainmakers?

Nature or nurture?
Are rainmakers born or is this something that, with the right understanding and training, can be built over time?

Interestingly, if we consider the historical professional career development within the legal sector, a solicitor is likely to be hired on their ability to produce high quantity, high quality work and advice. However, down the line when partnership roles are being considered, there is then a shift from work production to client development. But how does that shift take place, and are there elements of our character that can feed into that personal development?

There have been many insightful blogs and reports on particular personality traits that create the magical rainmaker combination. Harold Weinstein, previously chief operating officer of Caliper Corporation, identified three traits[1] where rainmakers consistently scored higher than their peers.

The first of these traits is the ego-drive. Whilst the "ego" trait is potentially not one that is considered to be a favorable asset, suggesting an egotistical, over-confident, and arrogant character, the ego-drive can be a strong business and rainmaker asset.

Being ego-driven doesn't necessarily mean that you have over-inflated self-esteem. In fact, when it comes to business, having a high ego-drive creates individuals with a passion to persuade and the self-motivated determination to succeed. When it comes to the ego-drive, being successful, creating the "win", doesn't stop with the financial reward. It goes deeper, more personal. The ego-drive thrives on the desire to "win" because of the sense of personal triumph and success that follows.

The concept of the ego-drive becomes very interesting when it sits alongside the next trait identified by Weinstein – empathy. This is the ability of the rainmaker to step into the client's shoes, to place themselves in their position, reflecting and considering a course of action from the perspective of the client. Focusing on the client's need and crafting the time to understand the client, their challenges, and desired outcomes creates sincerity, builds trust, and fosters an enduring relationship with the client.

The ego-empathy balance is a powerful pendulum that rainmakers seamlessly manage, creating a quality where rainmakers have the empathetic approach toward the client with the ego-driven desire to close the deal. This special relationship fosters success and delivers long-term business achievement.

What is the final, all important, string to the rainmaker bow? Resilience – potentially an unsurprising element of business personality. The ability to bounce back. Take the knock and come back stronger.

Within the constant evolution of the legal landscape, be that regulatory changes, government leadership, or new legislation, the rainmaker has the enviable ability to embrace and swiftly adapt to ride the waves of this landscape.

Resilience also plays a significant role in mental wellbeing. Faced with often tremendous stress, pressing deadlines, and the weight of responsibility, having the resilience to manage these external pressures and internal emotions is an asset that enables rainmakers to thrive.

If we are aware of the personality traits that create that magical rainmaker mix, we can feed this into our recruitment and selection process. No business wants, or needs, to be awash with rainmakers. There need to be other partners and solicitors who can continue the relationship and focus, diligently, on the task at hand. But, if we are adapting growth strategies or considering succession planning, being able to test for traits that have the potential to create rainmakers can be an incredibly valuable tool.

Be client-centric
Possibly an obvious suggestion is the concept that the client must be at the heart. So how does a rainmaker differentiate their client contact from other partners or fee-earners?

A rainmaker's relationships are genuine, solid, heartfelt connections. This client-centric approach is not built on disingenuous engagements – the rainmaker cares fully for the client, nurturing the relationship from the outset. The rainmaker becomes the confidante – a source that the client can trust and rely on, who then, in turn, provides a timely and responsive service, making them an invaluable asset.

Creating these meaningful relationships does not just involve professional awareness and understanding – it delves into their personal goals and ambitions. Blurring the personal and professional lines will help to deepen the connection and develop that advisor role, rather than adapting the role of a hired expert, which is a transactional function that doesn't evoke the emotional connection.

A rainmaker is apt at developing new ideas for the client, creatively looking for solutions and connections that will exceed expectation and deliver real value. Rainmakers are exceptional at embedding themselves into the fabric of the client's business, never losing track of a client's situation and creating a service that ensures loyalty and retention.

How else does a rainmaker create the holy grail of client connection? The art is in the ear. The power of listening – fully focused active listening. This is all about understanding the client, their problems and ambitions, and putting aside the desire to "push" a solution, product, or service, or waiting for the chance to jump in on the conversation. In fact, few of us really know how to listen, a skill that is not top of the leadership training program, but one that rainmakers excel in. It starts with asking an open-ended question and actively attending to the answer, reflecting and considering the client's content. Within the legal sector, and most professional services, the end goal is to provide advice and solutions, so taking the time to really listen to a client and their situation is a key element of the rainmaker and client relationship.

In an era where clients are becoming less loyal, more fluid in their buyer behavior, actively searching out better deals, regardless of previous performance, the ability of the rainmaker to retain clients becomes business-critical. The strength of the relationship between rainmaker and client is such that contact extends further than being a purely business transaction. The clients become brand ambassadors, advocating the firm to their networks, opening the door to their own client base, and creating a business development ripple effect.

Rainmakers have a hard balance when it comes to developing new client connections and servicing existing work and clients. I know that my reputation, and the reputation of Loch Associates, is only as good as the work that we do for our clients. Balancing the networking, the social media personality, and the future business planning whilst continually working on building a business is not an effortless task. It is very easy to get caught up chasing the new client, but you need to be careful. I would also recommend that the existing client comes first. Adopting a high-ranking client focus will, without a doubt, keep the business moving and going.

Prepare to plan
All hail to the ever-powerful plan! Rainmakers say goodbye to the "random acts of lunch", they steer away from mindless gathering of LinkedIn connections, they put down the scattergun of tactics. Instead, every target, interaction, and approach is considered and thoughtfully strategized to ensure every opportunity to optimize revenue is covered.

Rainmakers don't rely on organic business growth – they plan how to cultivate and build relationships that develop existing clients and bring in new prospects. The beginning process for business growth and development will be the identification of potential markets, geographical locations or sectors, fueled by detailed analysis. Priorities will be kept clear and then, with military precision, a plan drawn up to identify and target the key decision-makers and influencers, and engage and foster these new potential clients. These targets will always be based on genuine business alignment – reinforcing the client-centric approach.

Loch Associates Group is a much different business to the early days. Employment law services by their very nature can be tactical and one-off pieces of work, and I recognized that I needed to diversify the organization to deliver long-term growth, to future protect the peaks and troughs of work and income. Whilst providing HR support had always been a part of the Loch services, in 2014 I extended this offering further by adding in wellbeing and training services. Since then, we have added on business law and mediation services and immigration support. The development of the business, and the services that we provide, has always been driven by business data, whether that's considering the P&L of the business, or by looking at, and listening to, a client's needs.

Being data-driven individuals, rainmakers focus heavily on analysis to direct and orchestrate the plan. To this extent, the impact of a powerful CRM system can have a game-changing effect on not just client service but operational efficiency. These systems enable firms to understand their clients, their characteristics, behaviors, needs, and interactions to then inform future targeting.

Rainmakers are the beating heart of an organization – pumping life through all areas of its operation. They connect marketers and customer service departments, align fee-earners and forge the business' external reputational path, each step underpinned by an exacting strategy determining service excellence and unparalleled customer focus.

Focusing on the long-term benefit, the rainmaker plan doesn't rely on short-term gains. The identification of like-minded, value-based contacts that can drive future business and rewards is at the center of a rainmaker's plan. This means creating a circle of valuable future assets that have business development potential.

Be bold and be brave
The conventional path is not one that is followed by the rainmaker. The rainmaker has the courage to craft their own path, making bold and daring decisions along the way. They are the risk-taker of the organization, taking proactive steps in, sometimes, untouched territory.

To be bold and brave takes a leap of faith, to expose yourself and be vulnerable. In 2007, I stepped away from an equity partnership and made the decision to start up my own practice, a risky step that essentially saw me to some extent reinvent my career. Yes, I had a longstanding reputation as an employment lawyer but was suddenly propelled into the world of entrepreneurs, with the responsibility of building and developing a business sitting firmly at my door.

Being brave and carving a path was, and is, of critical importance for rainmakers, and along this route having the confidence to ask direct and sometimes challenging questions is critical.

When I decided to set up my own business, I had clients who had worked with me and wanted to stay with me when I made the move. This put me in the very fortunate position of having, to some extent, a ready-made client base with which to start my new business. However, unsurprisingly, there were restrictions that would have prevented me from "taking" those clients with me. I chose to have an open and honest conversation with the firm I was leaving and negotiate the terms of my exit. A bold step but one that was essential in ensuring my start-up would be viable from day one.

The rainmaker is highly visible. They have a presence that draws the attention of the room and creates an impact from the start, whether that's to their internal teams or to external connections. They have a personal brand that is, above all else, genuine. Bold leaders run a business with integrity, identifying what a business needs and taking the team on that transformational journey.

Create company collaboration
Culture is pivotal to creating a thriving and progressive organization and one that is led from the very top, from the rainmaker.

Understanding an organization's culture and how teams collaborate, share knowledge, and learn from each other is core to not just creating a successful rainmaker, but taking the organization on that journey to ensure long-term sustainable success.

One of the challenges I faced with managing more staff was maintaining the reputation and brand I'd carefully built as clients expected the same values and commercial, pragmatic advice, regardless of who was giving it. I cannot emphasize the importance of recruiting the right people for your business as this is so important to ensure the delivery of services matches the brand you have created. You need people who share your values, people you trust, and people who truly understand your vision for the business.

Team focus is absolutely critical to me, and I have embedded a team culture through everything we do, from training and onboarding of new staff to teambuilding events and activities. We work as a team and share in each other's success along the way.

A successful rainmaker will understand that the culture is bigger than just their personality – it needs to ripple through the whole organization, empowering, trusting, and encouraging all elements and areas of the business. The rainmaker may lead the charge but the troops behind are fully committed to the cause and the purpose.

Play the social strategy
The growth of social media has made it an essential component in the business development toolkit. Rainmakers have harnessed the full potential of these platforms to drive their profile and business to reach new audiences.

The ability of social media networks, specifically LinkedIn for the professional services sectors, to excel in lead generation makes it a critical path to increase reach and build and maintain relationships and connections without the need for real life engagement.

Every rainmaker will understand the potential of social media to identify and attract prospects, dismantling the geographical barriers that could previously hinder business development, but equally aware of the dangers it can present. Reputations can be damaged in as little as one post.

Used with seamless ease, a rainmaker won't just use social media to connect with people, but rather utilize these platforms to drive one of the most powerful business development tools – content. In a world that is awash with insight, creating compelling narratives that resonates with the reader, draws them in, and places them at the forefront of thought-leadership is fundamental to the rainmaker status.

Writing and contributing to articles was a key element of my success as an employment solicitor, setting me apart from the competition and reaffirming my area of expertise. In the early days, it was an essential route to awareness, and writing a piece on unpaid internships grabbed the attention of the local BBC Breakfast News, which then propelled me onto regional and national radio shows. It boosted my profile immeasurably.

A rainmaker utilizes the digital footprint of the organization to promote their thoughts and insight into industry topics, trends, and events. Social media posting and sharing is used to strengthen their standing in their field, but also deliver invaluable insight that educates potential clients and establishes themselves, and the wider firm, as thought-leaders and the go-to source for advice.

As top-performing leaders, rainmakers understand the ability of social media to drive the organization's professional brand, humanizing the firm and creating interactive engagement with a limitless audience. When executed with utter precision, a rainmaker utilizes the social sphere to extend their personas, to captivate audiences, and to reinforce their standing within their industry, amongst their peers, client connections, and potential prospects.

The feminine rainmaker
The role of women in legal leadership positions has taken great leaps in recent years, but there is still significant work to do to level out what is a very uneven playing field.

When I first set up the business, being a female entrepreneur was far more unusual compared to today, so much so that some people thought I was only doing it for pin money as a hobby. More than once, I attended an event or meeting with a male colleague, only for other attendees to assume he was my boss for no reason other than he was a man. Thankfully, the progress I have seen since I started my business in 2007 is staggering, but the challenge is still there.

With additional home pressures, it's no surprise that qualifying for rainmaker status often seems outside of the female grip, especially within firms that focus on billable hours and relentless client-focused networking and entertainment. But to harness the true potential of women lawyers, firms need to adapt their working practices, manage their expectations, and move away from a historically restrictive business model to ensure female entrepreneurs and future rainmakers have a pathway within the organization to develop and thrive.

In fact, should leaders be considering whether women possess an additional rainmaker asset, which many of their male counterparts lack? Women often have the ability to bring softer skills to the client relationship, to put a contact or client effortlessly at ease.

Interestingly, in the last year, we have seen a significant rise in female mentoring programs with the sole aim of enabling female lawyers to learn from leading rainmakers on topics that many of them face – such as imposter syndrome, the importance of internal and external networking, public speaking, and fear of "working the room".

The risk of burnout is much higher than it ever has been, and for a female leader balancing running their business with being a parent, wife, or partner at home, the lines have become very blurred. Rainmakers need to understand that it is just as important to take time for themselves. If you have built a team you can trust, you should be able to step away from the business to recharge.

The rainmakers name derives from the tribal proactive of rainmaking – the ability of an individual to create rain to enable crops to prosper. It makes sense then that a rainmaker role within an organization is one that focuses on business development to ensure the survival and future growth and success of the organization.

A rainmaker is a brilliant storyteller, crafting relevant content that motivates the receiver to connect on a deeper level, be that speaking at a conference, writing insightful blogs and articles, or networking at an industry event. They excel in business juggling, managing conflicting priorities, diary commitments, and workloads but ensuring that the client and the team are kept at the heart of the organization.

What hasn't changed since I set up Loch Associates is the interpersonal skills needed to be successful in business. Whether you are talking in person, on emails, over the phone, or on social media, people relate to people. Being genuine, having empathy, and approaching each day with sincerity will set you on the road to success.

References
1   www.lawyerbrain.com/wp-content/uploads/2023/04/caliper_herding_cats.pdf

Chapter 3:
Building reputation and relationships

By Susan Heaton-Wright, founder, Superstar Communicator

Building your professional reputation and relationships, both within your firm, industry, and with clients, is essential for your career and business success. But what is meant by reputation and relationships?

A professional reputation refers to the collective opinion or perception that others have of someone based on their behavior, actions, accomplishments, and interactions in a professional situation. It covers how you are perceived by colleagues, clients, employers, and the industry at large. A positive professional reputation can lead to opportunities such as job offers, promotions, partnerships, and collaborations, whilst a negative reputation could hinder career advancement and relationships. Building and maintaining a strong professional reputation often involves demonstrating integrity, trustworthiness, competence/ability, reliability, and proficiency in all aspects of work as a lawyer.

Why is professional reputation so important for lawyers?
In the competitive legal profession, professional reputation is particularly crucial for female lawyers for several reasons:

1. *Trust and credibility*. As lawyers, you rely heavily on trust and credibility in your interactions with clients, colleagues, support staff, the firm's partners, and other stakeholders. If these people trust you, they are more likely to confide in you and follow your advice. If they trust you, they are more likely to recommend you for more opportunities to build your skills and experience, internally and externally.
2. *Client referrals*. Having a strong positive reputation increases the chance of leads to client referrals and recommendations. Satisfied clients and senior colleagues are more inclined to recommend you to others, helping to expand your client base and business. In addition, senior colleagues are more likely to refer you for specific work or for promotion.

3. *Career advancement.* A good reputation has a positive impact on your career progression – it could open doors for career advancement. Opportunities include promotions within a law firm, the chance to work on specific cases or projects, increasing your skill set and experience, or invitations to join prestigious legal organizations. Within the legal profession, reputation and your business relationships are crucial in this area.
4. *Courtroom or legal effectiveness.* When representing a client, a lawyer's reputation can influence how they are perceived by judges, juries, and opposing counsel. A respected lawyer may find it easier to negotiate favorable settlements or persuade a judge or jury. The opposing team will anticipate your performance based on your reputation as a lawyer. A great reputation will challenge their perception of the case – the anticipated outcome – and undoubtedly impact their confidence.
5. *Ethical considerations.* Maintaining a solid reputation is often intertwined with ethical conduct. Lawyers are expected to adhere to high ethical standards and a tarnished reputation can raise doubts about integrity and professionalism. Women are held to higher ethical standards than men. Whilst this is wrong, it is something we should be aware of.
6. *Competitive advantage.* In a highly competitive legal landscape, a strong positive reputation can be a significant differentiator. Clients are more likely to choose a lawyer with a proven track record and positive reviews over one with a questionable reputation. Increasingly, clients are researching on review sites as well as asking for recommendations from friends.
7. *Risk management.* A good reputation can act as a buffer against potential risks and controversies. Clients and employers are more likely to stand by a lawyer with a history of ethical conduct and professionalism during challenging times. Although there is an adage that you are only as good as your last case, if there is a controversy, your previous reputation will also work in your favor (unless, of course, it is gross misconduct).

In summary, a lawyer's professional reputation is instrumental in building trust, attracting clients, advancing their career, navigating legal challenges effectively, and upholding ethical standards. It's a critical asset that requires careful cultivation and maintenance throughout one's legal career.

What are business relationships?
Business relationships are connections between individuals, companies, or organizations that involve interactions, transactions, collaborations, or partnerships aimed at achieving common goals or mutual benefits. These relationships can take various forms and may include the following.

1. *Supplier and vendor relationships.* These are relationships between a business and its suppliers or vendors who provide goods or services necessary for the business operations. Building strong relationships with suppliers can lead to better pricing, reliable deliveries, and improved product quality. In a legal context, this might be bringing in expert witnesses or specialized research to support a case.

2. *Customer relationships.* These are relationships between a business and its customers or clients. Developing positive relationships with customers is crucial for customer retention, loyalty, and repeat business. It involves effective communication, meeting customer needs, providing excellent service, and addressing concerns promptly. Personally, I believe that customers should feel valued and "loved" – they should know that you value their custom, are contactable, and deliver effectively. There are often conversations where individuals request recommendations for specific services – which include recommendations for lawyers. Discussions include, "Don't touch ABC firm" as much as "Go to XYZ; they were brilliant". Word of mouth and recommendations are very powerful – if you build good relationships with your clients you are more likely to win future business. I do appreciate that the profession often works with a "billable time" model – however, time spent emailing confirmation of a task with a client, who has chased you, is not only billable, but part of the lawyer/client relationship.

3. *Partnerships and collaborations.* Businesses often form partnerships or collaborate with other entities to leverage each other's strengths, resources, and expertise. This could include joint ventures, strategic alliances, or collaborations on specific projects or initiatives. For example, a business contact of mine is a high-end wealth manager, providing advice for high value women to plan their finances post-divorce. She has developed strategic alliances with highly reputable law firms, to provide additional services for clients. If you have a good reputation, you could approach equally highly respected professionals to collaborate and offer a range of services to clients that are mutually beneficial to both businesses.

Chapter 3: Building reputation and relationships

4. *Employee relations.* Businesses also have relationships with their employees. A positive work environment, fair compensation, opportunities for growth, and effective communication contribute to strong employee relations, leading to higher productivity, morale, and retention rates. Being named a Top 500 best company to work with by *The Times*, or the Top 500 Law Firms to work at, attracts highly talented candidates for job opportunities. From an employee's perspective, working for a highly respected firm is valuable for their own career development.
5. *Government and regulatory relationships.* Businesses interact with government agencies, regulators, and policymakers. Compliance with regulations, lobbying efforts, and advocacy for favorable policies are part of managing these relationships. The Law Society regulates behavior within the profession. It is unlikely that any lawyer wishes to be disciplined or even struck off by the Law Society. Being aware of professional standards is crucial.
6. *Competitor relationships.* While businesses compete with each other, they also have relationships with competitors. This may involve industry collaborations, market positioning strategies, or monitoring competitive dynamics to stay informed and agile. For example, negotiating between opposing sides on a case to avoid going to court is easier if both sides respect each other's reputation and have built a relationship of mutual respect.

Building and maintaining healthy business relationships requires trust, communication, mutual respect, integrity, and a focus on creating value for all parties involved. Good relationships can lead to opportunities for growth, innovation, and long-term success.

Why do they differ to personal relationships?
Business relationships differ from personal relationships primarily due to their purpose, context, and dynamics. Here are some key differences:
1. *Purpose.* The primary purpose of business relationships is typically to achieve specific business goals, such as generating revenue, improving efficiency, expanding market reach, or creating value for stakeholders. In contrast, personal relationships focus more on emotional connection, support, companionship, and personal fulfilment.
2. *Formality.* Business relationships often have a formal structure with

defined roles, responsibilities, and expectations. They may involve contracts, agreements, and legal frameworks to ensure clarity and accountability. Personal relationships, on the other hand, are often based on informal interactions, shared experiences, and emotional bonds.

3. *Boundaries.* Business relationships tend to have clearer boundaries compared to personal relationships. There is a delineation between professional interactions and personal life, although building rapport and trust are still important in business settings. In personal relationships, boundaries can be more fluid and based on individual preferences and comfort levels.

4. *Communication style.* Communication in business relationships is often more structured, professional, and goal-oriented. It may involve formal meetings, presentations, reports, and emails aimed at achieving business objectives. Personal relationships, on the other hand, involve more informal and personal communication styles, including casual conversations, sharing feelings, and personal challenges. With personal relationships you have a higher level of trust.

5. *Decision-making.* Business relationships often involve decision-making based on strategic considerations, financial analysis, market trends, benefits, and risk assessment. Decisions may be made collectively by teams or based on organizational priorities. In personal relationships, decisions are typically based on emotions, personal values, and individual preferences.

6. *Duration and stability.* Business relationships can vary in duration and stability based on business needs, market conditions, and industry dynamics. They may evolve, adapt, or end based on changing circumstances. Personal relationships, especially close friendships and family bonds, often have a longer-term outlook with a focus on mutual support and enduring connections.

7. *Conflict resolution.* In business relationships, conflict resolution often follows formal processes, such as mediation, negotiation, or arbitration, especially when contractual obligations are involved. Personal relationships may rely more on empathy, compromise, and understanding to resolve conflicts and maintain harmony.

While there can be overlap or similarities in how people approach building trust, communication, and mutual respect in both personal and business relationships, the underlying objectives and contexts significantly differentiate the two types of relationships.

Building reputation
Building reputation and relationships is crucial for career development for female lawyers for several reasons:
1. *Networking opportunities.* Reputation and relationships open doors to building your network. This could mean attending conferences, joining professional organizations, or even meeting other legal professionals in your area. Networking could lead to new clients, mentorship opportunities, and collaborations on cases. If you are known within your own community – either personally or in the business community – you are more likely to pick up business or be referred for business.
2. *Client trust.* Building a strong reputation helps in developing and gaining trust from clients. When potential clients see that you have a good reputation in the legal community, they are more likely to trust your expertise and hire you for their legal needs.
3. *Career advancement.* Reputation and relationships play a significant role in career advancement. Being well-connected can lead to recommendations for promotions, partnerships, or opportunities to work on high-profile cases. Also, if you have worked with a very prestigious or highly regarded firm, or even a case, this could build your reputation for future career progression.
4. *Setting yourself up as a subject expert.* Personally, I believe this is an excellent way to build your reputation. This could include writing specific articles, sharing your expertise by presenting to business groups or your colleagues, being a panelist at an event, or even a speaker at a conference. For all these activities, I recommend you have a discussion with your marketing department to see if there are opportunities to share your expertise. It is possible they will have a list of potential speakers for events, or employees happy to write articles. There could be some excellent opportunities for you to be involved in.
5. *Knowledge sharing.* Building relationships with other legal professionals allows for knowledge sharing. This could include staying updated on legal trends and changes, learning from others' experiences, or even finding new strategies for handling cases. The local law society is an excellent place to do this, where you could be known

within your own legal community. Attending seminars and conferences as part of your professional development is crucial.

6. *Mentorship and support*. Having a good reputation and strong relationships can also lead to mentorship opportunities. Female lawyers may benefit from mentorship from more experienced lawyers who can provide guidance, support, and advice on navigating the legal profession. I strongly recommend you ask if there is already a mentoring scheme in your firm. If there is a specific person you would like to mentor you, why not approach them? Be very clear, such as, "Do you have 15 minutes where I could ask you a specific question". Everyone is busy and receiving a random, "Please could you mentor me" request is less likely to be successful. There are also huge benefits to being a mentor to other women.

7. *Business development*. For female lawyers who may be considering starting their own practice or moving into leadership positions, reputation and relationships are essential for business development. Building a network of clients, colleagues, and mentors can help in growing a successful legal practice or advancing within a firm. I would also recommend you build business relationships with senior women in other professions. Sharing challenges as a leader with women in other professions is enlightening and could provide an alternative perspective.

8. *Visibility and recognition*. A strong reputation can lead to increased visibility and recognition within the legal community. This could mean being invited to speak at conferences, receiving awards and accolades, or being featured in industry publications – all of which can further enhance your career opportunities. But don't forget to have a conversation with your marketing department to see if there are ways they could support you in gaining visibility and recognition.

Overall, building reputation and relationships is a strategic investment in one's career as a woman lawyer, helping to open doors, gain trust, access resources, and ultimately advance professionally.

Why don't women do this?
There are several factors that could be stopping women from prioritizing building reputation and relationships as much as they should in their legal careers.

1. *Societal expectations.* Societal norms and expectations often place a heavier burden on women to balance career and family responsibilities. This can lead to less time and energy available for networking and relationship-building activities. There are many opportunities for people to network after work, but for many women who have family caring responsibilities, access to these events is limited. Some firms and organizations now schedule lunchtime events to increase access.
2. *Workplace dynamics.* In some legal environments, particularly those with male-dominated cultures, women may face barriers to networking and building relationships. They may not have the same access to informal networks or may feel excluded from networking opportunities, such as client events at the golf club or weekend sporting events. As I have previously mentioned, if you have family commitments – and of course men have these too – you might be excluded from these opportunities to network.
3. *Confidence and self-promotion.* Research shows that women tend to be less confident in self-promotion compared to men.[1] They may downplay their achievements or hesitate to advocate for themselves, which can impact their ability to build a strong reputation.
4. *Implicit bias.* Gender biases and stereotypes can also come into play, affecting how women are perceived and treated in professional settings. This can impact their opportunities for networking, mentorship, and career advancement. Mary Ann Sieghart's groundbreaking book *The Authority Gap*[2] highlights the challenges successful women still experience. A woman must work harder to prove her expertise and knowledge compared to a similarly qualified man.
5. *Lack of role models.* A lack of visible female role models in leadership positions within the legal profession can make it challenging for women to envision and pursue career paths that involve building reputation and relationships effectively. Although there are more women in senior roles, this is not the norm. Aspiration and seeing more senior women is a significant motivator for younger women to aspire to.
6. *Time constraints.* Balancing demanding workloads, client responsibilities, and personal commitments can leave little time for networking and relationship-building activities. Women may prioritize immediate tasks over long-term career development strategies. Being aware of this is key. Blocking out even an hour a week of non-billable time to specif-

ically focus on relationship-building activities, whether in-person or online, would be hugely beneficial.
7. *Access to resources.* Historically, women have had limited access to resources such as mentorship programs, networking events, and professional development opportunities, which can hinder their ability to build relationships and establish a strong reputation. However, increasingly, firms are organizing women's networks to address specific support talented women require. There are also larger groups for female lawyers such as Women in the Law[3] and The Female Lawyer Breakfast Networking,[4] providing opportunities for female talent to network and build further knowledge and support.

Addressing these challenges requires a multi-faceted approach that includes promoting diversity and inclusion in the legal profession, providing support and resources for women, challenging gender biases and stereotypes, and creating more equitable opportunities for networking and career advancement.

Here are some ideas on how you can build your reputation and business relationships.
1. *Attend networking events.* Try to attend legal conferences, seminars, and networking events, both within your firm and in the broader legal community. These events provide opportunities to meet other legal professionals, potential clients, and mentors. Ask if you could attend these events to represent the firm or chamber. If you have limited time due to family commitments, why not try a "drop in" lunchtime event. One senior lawyer I have worked with has created an informal lunchtime network, where anyone available will meet for lunch at a specific restaurant. There is no judgement if you are unable to attend due to workload, but it is an effective way to maintain relationships and have a support network.
2. *Join professional organizations.* Become a member of professional organizations relevant to your legal practice area, chambers, or interests. These organizations often host networking events, offer mentorship programs, and provide resources for career development. This could provide an opportunity for you to be a panelist or speaker where you demonstrate your expertise. The local Chamber of Commerce is an excellent way to build your reputation.
3. *Participate in the Law Society and other legal associations/networks.*

Get involved in local or national associations related to your practice area. Law associations often have committees, events, and networking opportunities that can help you connect with peers and build your reputation. You could raise your visibility this way.
4. *Utilize social media.* Leverage social media platforms like LinkedIn to showcase your expertise, share legal insights, and connect with other professionals in your field. Engage in discussions, join relevant groups, and publish articles or posts to enhance your visibility. I have mentioned before that the marketing department of your firm or chambers could be looking for individuals to write articles. Check to see what successes you could share (case-wise) because these posts and case studies are excellent proof of your capabilities. The marketing department should have a marketing plan – you could volunteer to provide content when you attend events and share successes.
5. *Seek mentorship.* I have mentioned before about the value of mentors. These provide insight and an unbiased opinion. Identify experienced lawyers, both male and female, who can serve as mentors and provide guidance on career development. Mentorship relationships can offer valuable insights, support, and networking opportunities. Remember, there is huge value that can be gained from being a mentor as well as a mentee.
6. *Attend continuing education programs.* Part of your continuous professional development is to remain up to date on legal trends and developments by attending continuing education programs, webinars, and workshops. These events not only expand your knowledge but also provide opportunities to network with industry experts.
7. *Volunteer for speaking engagements.* Offer to speak at conferences, seminars, or legal panels on topics related to your expertise. Speaking engagements can enhance your credibility, visibility, and reputation within the legal community. As well as solo speaking engagements, being a panelist as an expert is very important. It increases your visibility and builds trust. Local schools and business groups also welcome speakers. Schools have career fairs and events for their students. Welcoming a lawyer to speak provides huge value to their events – and it is "newsworthy" within your firm or chambers.
8. *Build relationships with clients.* Focus on building strong relationships with your clients by providing excellent legal services, maintaining open communication, and demonstrating your commitment to their

success. Satisfied clients become valuable sources of referrals and testimonials. Never underestimate the power of a satisfied client.
9. *Collaborate with peers*. Collaborate with other lawyers within your firm or chambers on cases or projects whenever possible. Working collaboratively fosters professional relationships, expands your network, and showcases your ability to work effectively in teams. This is particularly powerful when you work with senior leaders – they could be influential in identifying future talent.
10. *Seek feedback*. Regularly seek feedback from colleagues, mentors, and clients to assess your strengths, areas for improvement, and overall reputation. Use feedback to continuously refine your skills and enhance your professional image. Feedback occasionally has negative connotations. Many of us have experienced poorly delivered feedback – either it has been given at the wrong time or it focused on the negatives rather than constructive feedback. If you have a good relationship with a mentor, a line manager or a colleague, you could ask for honest feedback.

By implementing these strategies, you can proactively build your reputation, expand your network, and create opportunities for career advancement as a female lawyer. However, I suspect you are looking at this content and thinking, "How on earth do I do all this? How many hours do I need?"

Planning and effort

Building your reputation and business relationships involves a plan and consistent effort. If you are time poor due to family commitments, even allocating one hour a week to your career development will be valuable to you. Here are some steps to consider.
1. *Define your goals*. Start by defining your goals and objectives. What do you want to achieve in terms of reputation building and business relationships? Do you want to reach a specific career level? Specialize in a specific area? Work with particular teams? Set specific, measurable, and realistic goals to guide your efforts.
2. *Identify your target audience*. Identify the target audience and influencers relevant to your career. These could include the senior people in your firm or chambers or key members within your Inn if you are a barrister, but it could also include clients, colleagues, industry peers, influencers, potential partners, and decision-makers.

3. *Understand your value proposition.* If you are wishing to progress to more senior positions, being clear on what you bring to the firm or chambers in the way of generated income, reputation, and expertise is essential. Clearly articulate your value proposition – what sets you apart, your expertise, skills, strengths, and what value you bring to the firm or chambers. This will form the basis of your reputation and how you position yourself.
4. *Build a strong online presence.* In today's digital age, having a strong online presence is crucial. Ensure you check your firm's social media rules first. Optimize your LinkedIn profile and engage in social media platforms relevant to your industry. As mentioned before, contribute to articles that will be published online.
5. *Networking and relationship building.* Actively network and build relationships with industry professionals, clients, and peers. Attend networking events, conferences, seminars, and participate in industry associations or forums. If there are speakers you like, follow up – connect with them on LinkedIn to see what other relevant content they create. Follow up with contacts and maintain regular communication.
6. *Provide value and share knowledge.* Demonstrate your expertise and provide value to your network by sharing relevant content, insights, and resources. This could include writing articles, blogs, giving presentations, or participating in panel discussions. Also be a mentor to more junior colleagues.
7. *Seek mentorship and guidance.* Seek mentorship from experienced professionals who can offer guidance, advice, and support in navigating your career path and building your reputation. Mentors provide valuable insights and help you expand your network.
8. *Deliver exceptional service.* As a lawyer, focus on delivering exceptional service and exceeding client expectations. Positive client experiences and testimonials contribute significantly to building your reputation. Never underestimate this.
9. *Seek feedback and improve continuously.* Solicit feedback from clients, colleagues, and mentors to identify areas for improvement. Use constructive feedback to refine your skills, enhance your offerings, and strengthen your reputation over time. Take your appraisals seriously – be prepared with examples of the work you have been involved in and seek feedback and advice on how to progress in your career.
10. *Maintain integrity and professionalism.* Uphold high ethical standards,

integrity, and professionalism in all your interactions as a lawyer. Trust and credibility are foundational to building a positive reputation and long-lasting business relationships.

Consistency, persistence, and a proactive mindset are key to successfully building your reputation and business relationships. It's an ongoing process that requires continuous effort, learning, and adaptation to succeed in today's competitive legal landscape. I wish you every success in continuing to work on your mindset and building these essential business relationships with others.

References
1. *Gender Gap in Self Promotion*, by Christine L. Exley and Judd Kessler, National Bureau of Economic research 2021. www.nber.org/papers/w26345
2. www.maryannsieghart.com/the-authority-gap/
3. www.womeninthelawuk.com/
4. www.eventbrite.co.uk/e/female-lawyer-breakfast-networking-flbn-tickets-807602981257

Chapter 4:
Networking effectively and positively at events

By Joanna Gaudoin, Inside Out Image

Very few people, including lawyers, genuinely enjoy going to networking events. It feels uncomfortable and many associate it directly with selling. Networking is a time-intensive activity, a skill, and isn't the reason most lawyers become lawyers.

Being able to network effectively and positively at events is, however, an important if not vital skill. When you have the ability to do it well, it will help your confidence, and in time and with practice you will become far more comfortable and effective so you see positive outcomes that in themselves will encourage and motivate you.

This chapter looks at:
- The value of networking, particularly for business development;
- How to plan to network well;
- How to approach events, including the skills you need; and
- What to do after an event – after all, if you do nothing you have wasted your time.

The value of networking
Individuals often associate networking solely with business development – to bring in new work. That is a very good reason, both to meet new potential clients and intermediaries and deepen relationships with existing clients and contacts. Indeed, networking is essential if you have a business development responsibility. It is the quickest way to meet a variety of people who could be prospective clients or referrers in any one unit of time. Assuming you select the most suitable events, it is also the easiest way to start to build a relationship with them by building rapport, credibility, and trust. From there, you can continue to build relationships with the people who you think are most suitable and valuable to have in your network.

Even if you don't have direct responsibility for business development at the moment, assuming you want to progress your career, then you are likely to one day. The earlier you start to build a network and develop these skills, the easier that will be in terms of being used to doing it and having an existing network. After all, you can't just build a network when you need one.

Additionally, there are other reasons to network, beyond creating a personal profile and building relationships for the purpose of business development. These reasons include:
- To stay up to date with the market in terms of:
  - Legal developments;
  - The competition; and
  - Understanding your clients' circumstances and challenges better.
- To support your own development – networking events often have speakers on both technical and soft skill topics.
- To have a network for when you want or need to look for a new role. Networks are often excellent places to hear about new potential roles.

It is also relevant to consider that the first two reasons above support business development too, as they help you to increase your knowledge and skills. This is valuable to your network, including prospective clients and referrers, and helps you build credibility, confidence, and the skills to engage effectively with others.

Networking is a long-term game and isn't just about the people you meet directly.

Developing a strategy and plan

Time is limited so it is important to use your time well. If you put the time into thinking through your networking strategy and plan, it will make decisions about what to attend easier and will be more likely to lead to good outcomes that will keep you motivated and invested in the plan. Networking is a long game as relationships take time to build and it is a career-long activity.

The earlier you can start in your career, the easier it will be to build your skills (as well as your network!) and start reaping the benefits. It is also likely to support accelerated career progression, if that is what you want.

When starting to work on your networking strategy and plan, there are two key questions to reflect on:
- Why do you want to build a network by attending events?
- Who do you want to meet to fulfil that goal?

These will help you decide what sorts of events to attend. For instance, if your goals are predominantly around learning, then legal conferences are likely to be a good type of event. However, if business development is your focus, then finding events that your prospective clients and/or potential referrers/intermediaries attend will be the key goal.

At this planning stage, it is a good idea to think realistically as to how many events you might be able to commit to in a month. It's better to commit to fewer events and to actually attend and build a solid foundation, rather than making an unrealistic plan, failing to keep up to it, and losing motivation for the whole plan.

Regular events can be great to attend – reconnecting with people you already know is often underrated, but this is how trust is developed and deeper relationships are more likely to lead to business opportunities. The other benefit of a regular event is you always know when it is, so it's easier to plan for and commit to. Even regular events you attend will generally have new visitors so there is often the opportunity to broaden your network, as well as deepen it.

Other considerations for which events to attend:

- *Time of day.* If you aren't a morning person or prefer to get client work done before any networking events, then avoiding breakfast events will be important. Likewise, considering whether you will get away from work to attend a lunchtime event or have the energy and time amongst personal commitments to make an evening one are also valid considerations.
- *Location.* If an evening event is far away from either your office or home, you are less likely to actually go unless there is a standout benefit. Consider which locations are best for you, together with whether the sort of people you want to meet will be there.
- *Format.* Events that have a focus such as a presentation can make it psychologically easier to attend, as it feels like there is a natural topic of conversation. If you are new to attending networking events and/or nervous then this can be a good option. If you feel confident and want to maximize conversation opportunities, then events with no precise format and lots of people in a room are a great choice.

It is best to try a range of events and see what suits you in terms of outcomes (remembering it's a long game). Finding events can feel challenging if you aren't already attending them. Online research can be fruitful. Additionally, asking the marketing or business development departments at your firm (if it has them) can be helpful as they often have an events calendar and list. Otherwise, asking trusted contacts and colleagues what they attend can be another way to find events that may suit you.

It's best to attend an event a few times before deciding whether it is one to continue with. The biggest advantage to networking at well-publicized events is that, once you get to know people, you get invitations to less-publicized events, which is highly beneficial. At those events, there is a greater degree of immediate trust as everyone knows that the individuals attending have been personally invited. An example of this could be an accountant's drinks event. If an accountant is a good referrer for you, this could be a great opportunity to meet their clients.

Many people, including lawyers, underestimate the importance of being known broadly internally. There is a key business development reason for lawyers – cross-selling. Many don't make the most of this opportunity. It is such an easy win to have clients engage your law firm for one service and then to pass them to others for other instructions. Naturally, this relies on them being happy with the initial service and there being enough of a relationship so that the first lawyer is aware of other challenges. However, often the biggest barrier is lawyers not knowing their colleagues well enough to refer within the firm and so not wanting to risk referring their valuable client to a colleague they don't know, like, and trust. Networking internally means you can get to know lawyers in other parts of your firm, refer work, and even work collaboratively on how you could make this happen more proactively and frequently. Therefore, it is worth making time to attend internal networking events. If they don't exist, suggest the idea or start them yourself.

Preparing to go to events

Once you have a strategy and plan, this will hopefully mean you have registered to attend some events and have them firmly in your diary.

It's always valuable to understand the format of each event you are attending. Many are flexible but some have a talk or expect each guest to speak briefly. There's nothing worse for your confidence than thinking the event has a relaxed start time and turning up halfway through an activity of some kind, so find out what the format is.

It is essential to have advanced notice of whether you will be asked to say anything in front of the group to introduce yourself and what you do, as it's rarely a good surprise. If this is the norm at an event then it will usually only be for one to two minutes, but in that time, you need to get people's attention and be someone they want to speak to later on during the event.

If you do need to speak for a minute or two, consider who the likely audience is. People who will understand easily what you do or not? I find a helpful format for this kind of introduction is to:
- Say who you are;
- Say where you are from;
- Give a brief outline about what you do; and
- Bring it to life with a recent, anonymous, and short case study.

By doing this you can explain what sorts of problems you help to resolve for clients and/or the benefits you bring. Fundamentally, that is what nearly everyone does in some regard when you analyze the work you do. When people understand this, as well as how you approached the work and the outcome you achieved, it is easier for them to know whether you could assist them or anyone else they know.

When planning what you will say, think about the "how" too. You need to be loud enough so people can hear, but not too loud so you're shouting. You need to speak slowly, clearly, and with some variation in tone so people can digest what you're saying and remain attentive and engaged.

Whilst the need to give this longer group introduction to yourself is relatively uncommon, you will definitely need to introduce yourself in smaller groups or pairs. Giving a job title is rarely a good way to do this. Why? Because it is uninteresting, and the other person may have certain preconceptions about what you do and switch off. Instead, it is best to come up with a couple of phrases that fundamentally explain:
- Who you help – be specific, e.g. people with a lot of assets;
- With what – the problem you solve/benefit you bring;
- When – in what situation; and
- By – an explanation of what you do for them.

This will likely need to be adapted according to whom you are speaking, but these elements should form the building blocks. It is worth practicing it in a normal tone that doesn't sound rehearsed.

A further pre-event activity you may want to try is to review the guest list, if one has been supplied in advance. This will help you think more about who is there, any people you might want to try and meet (without scouring the room for them), as well as identifying anybody you have met before. It can be good to drop a short message to such people, saying you are looking forward to seeing them. It will make it easier to speak again at the event as well as help your confidence and potentially theirs.

It can also be helpful to have some broad goals for each event that you go to. Those could be as high level as "Speak to five people", or "Arrange a further meeting with these two people". This will help you focus, and you are likely to achieve more from the event than you would have done without thinking about what you'd like to achieve. It can also be a bargaining tool with yourself: "I can leave when…".

Attending an event

Many people approach networking events under a cloud of pressure – to bring in new work, to be liked, to stay for at least two hours. It might sound easy to say but these sorts of pressures won't help.

What is more likely to help is to think about meeting some people with the goal of getting to know them a little and to find out about one another's work. Another opportunity to look out for is whether you can help them at all. This doesn't necessarily need to be about work directly but can include interesting and helpful resources, or telling them about other events worth attending. Helping others is not only personally fulfilling but will help you stay top of mind with that person and make them more willing to help you when you need it.

Another helpful reflection can be to consider other circumstances when you have built new relationships. Maybe when collecting your child from school? At the gym? On a charity or school committee? There is no reason why this is any different at a networking event – everyone is still human. Simply, there is a business purpose and everyone is attending for that reason. The more you can consider how to connect with people, enjoy what you learn, and repeat it more frequently, the easier networking will become. Even when we feel people are very different to us, there is usually some point of commonality to be found.

It might sound simple, but always plan your journey thoroughly to get to an event, making sure the event is where you think it is and considering your travel options. A stressful journey and being late don't make for a calm, confident arrival at an event. I once sat next to somebody who had had an awful morning pre-event, including multiple transport issues. Not only was she late, but in downloading all her troubles, she didn't get off to the best start with those of us sitting at her table. What energy do you want to bring to the conversations you have? I'm not suggesting you should be fake and inauthentic, but think about what impact you want to have on others and how to be the best version of your professional self. What do you want to be remembered for?

Arriving on time or early for the event can be very helpful. This might be the opposite to what you naturally want to do. The reason this is helpful is that it can feel less daunting than walking into a room full of people where conversations are already in full swing. Often, when arriving early, there will be more opportunities to talk to the host and they may even introduce you to some people directly.

Getting into conversation can feel like a big challenge. Choosing who to speak to at an event is of pivotal importance. Assuming that just walking up to anyone to join them is a good strategy could lead to not only a frosty reception but a knock to your confidence. Neither of which are the best basis for starting to build a relationship!

To give yourself the time to decide which person or people to join, take the time to get a drink when you arrive at an event. Not only can it help your confidence to have that coffee/tea/water/wine in one hand, but it gives you an opportunity to look around and see where you might head. You don't want to end up standing in the middle of the room looking lost. You may also get talking to someone whilst getting a drink, which can be a nice, easy start to the event.

If this doesn't happen and you need to join others elsewhere, then you need to look for an easy space for you to move into. As a guide, if two people are stood directly opposite one another with their feet parallel to one another, that is usually a sign they are in deep conversation and not open to new people joining them. Conversely, if they are stood more alongside one another, there's an easy space for you to fit into.

Uneven groups often work well too. It is rare that a conversation is balanced and even in this scenario, so joining and potentially "rescuing" someone from a conversation they are less involved in can be a good move.

Large groups are rarely good to join unless you know at least one person well and are sure they will be pleased to see you. Conversely, people on their own can be excellent people to approach. Even if they are on their phone, they are unlikely to be doing something important if they are in the main networking area. Often, they are nervous and trying to occupy themselves. This means they will usually be very happy if someone approaches them.

If you are attending an event with colleagues, try to avoid staying together. It can be overwhelming for the people you meet, and it means you diminish the number of people you meet as a firm. The only exception to this is if you had planned to introduce a colleague to someone specific or are taking a junior person with you to learn about networking skills.

Once you have chosen who to approach, you need to start to engage. You will have heard all that is said about first impressions. They are very important at networking as people have a choice whether to engage with you and for how long. If you impact them negatively, they may choose to make a quick exit.

What to avoid:
- Shaking their hand far too strongly or weakly.
- Giving them a business card immediately.
- Making "What do you do?" your first question.
- Dominating the conversation to focus on yourself, especially if they are already speaking to someone else.

Fundamentally, when you introduce yourself to someone, you want them to feel important and that you are interested in them. After all, that is the main challenge with networking at events and in fact many human interactions – being interested and interesting.

Good eye contact, a smile, and a clear pronunciation of your name make for a great to start to a conversation. Unless you join an individual, you will always be interrupting! People won't be stood there in silence. As long as you consider the body language, including whether the group is "open", there won't be an issue. However, personally, I don't like to feel I am disrupting a conversation so I will wait for a lull in the conversation, introduce myself, but invite them to continue their conversation and say I will join in. Some will accept that invitation, and others will take the opportunity to start a new one to include you!

Following that, I would suggest there are four key conversation stages to get through:
1. *General conversation*. Getting into sharing work information too soon is unnatural – having a more general conversation on points of commonality helps you to get to know one another a little and starts to build trust. Many people dislike small talk but at least some is key to start to build rapport. Simple topics such as whether someone has come to the event before, how they got there, and how they heard

about it can be good conversation starters that are likely to lead into broader conversations. Remember to listen out for and give "hooks". This means someone mentioning something you could ask someone more about and you doing the same for them. You don't want to miss this stage, but you equally don't want to stay on it for the entire conversation.

2. *Ask them about their work.* It's best if you can get them to speak about their work first – it shows interest/politeness and helps you to know their situation, and therefore how best to talk about what you do and anything that might be particularly worth focusing on when you speak about your work. For instance, if you are speaking to an accountant who might be a good referrer, you might later talk about some work you are doing that came through an accountant to help the person make the link in their mind. At this stage, be curious about this person's work – try and gain greater clarification on what it is and show interest in them and what they enjoy most about their work.

3. *Talk about your work.* This is your turn to be interesting and use some of the preparation you did. Ideally, you want someone to be interested enough to ask questions. Avoid jargon and watch people's body language to check they are engaged and following what you are saying. Make sure your body language is open and you are making good eye contact. You can't make someone stay focused on what you are saying but considering your body language, how you speak, and what you say will all help.

4. *Conclude the conversation.* At events, you want to balance quantity and quality of conversations. Whilst you don't want to just have one conversation with someone you connected well with all evening, you don't want to have lots of very short conversations where no real connection was made. It's always good to leave a conversation on a high, before you have both run out of things to say. It then creates the opportunity to have a follow up call or coffee. Legal matters often involve a degree of emotion, whether business or personal, so building rapport and trust with a potential client or referrer is well worth the effort.

Whilst your focus should be on the people you are with and listening attentively, if you notice an individual near you who looks lost then try to make a space for them and gesture for them to join. It's a kind behavior but also helps you make a positive impact on another person. Taking opportunities to build relationships and be positively memorable are key when networking.

An often-overlooked point is when to mention if you can help with something the other person mentions. It's always best to avoid jumping in the minute they mention it as this can look overly keen and pushy. You may wish to mention it later in the conversation, linking it to what they said. If it is directly related to the services you offer, you need to be even more careful to avoid looking pushy, which may involve raising it in a follow-up email or conversation. Not only does this avoid you looking like you are pushing your own agenda, but it also implies that you have continued to think of that person even after the event.

If you think you have a useful connection for them, always give the caveat that you need to check with the other person first to make the best use of everyone's time. If you don't take the time to do this, you can cause awkwardness and embarrassment amongst the people you introduce to one another. Individuals may have no idea for what purpose you are introducing them when they get the connection email.

Leaving people and moving on
It's important to talk to a variety of people during the event so there will come a point where you need to move on. In a group, this is easy. You might want to reiterate any next steps you agreed with individuals, so they are easier for you to act on afterwards and to remind the person. For others, it is valuable to ask if they are on LinkedIn and, assuming they confirm, then ask for their details (if you don't already have them on a business card or won't remember their name from their badge).

Which raises another important point – business cards. Some people consider these outdated and not environmentally-friendly. However, I think they are highly useful. It means that, following the event, it is a lot easier to consider who you spoke to and build on any next steps. You also have more details than LinkedIn is likely to provide, assuming they are on there.

Naturally, you could connect immediately on LinkedIn using your phone at the time. However, there are two issues with this – firstly and importantly, the minute you get your phone out there is distraction away from the person you are speaking to. You might see an important message from your other half or an interesting social media post by a good friend and have your attention momentarily drawn away. Not good for the person you are talking to as they will lose your attention. The other factor is remembering the next day who you connected with and what the next action is, if any. Having a tangible card can be far more helpful.

Make sure you have the information you want before you leave people and ensure they feel that you enjoyed talking to them. With a group, saying you are going to go and get another drink or speak to a certain person is absolutely fine. With an individual, less so. Leaving someone on their own is rarely a kind behavior – even the most confident people often feel a bit nervous at networking. You want to avoid undoing a positive "relationship building" conversation..

A good way to move on is to say to the person it's been great chatting to them, but you should probably both meet some more people and look for a group together you could join. Another way is to suggest you both go and get another drink. Then you may get talking to new people, either together or separately. If you really need to go to the bathroom, leaving your drink with the person can be a good way to reassure them you are coming back and it will make sure you do. If on that walk to the bathroom someone starts to speak to you, explain you are mid-conversation and invite them to join you. If you know them already, you could say you will find them later on.

Another way to avoid leaving someone alone if you need to leave or need to speak to someone else before the end of the event is by being upfront with the person you were speaking to, explaining you don't want to leave them on their own and suggesting you both join another group first.

After an event

If you don't do anything following an event, you have wasted your time. It breaks trust if you have committed to following up with someone – a high proportion of people fall into this category. If someone doesn't send you an article link they said that they would, then would they do a good job for you, if you engaged them?

Ideally within 24 hours, consider who you met at the event and what follow-up is required. The minimum should be a connection request on LinkedIn. LinkedIn can serve as a business address book, with its excellent search function – it is easy to find someone even if you can't remember their full name as long as you remember some other facts about them such as company or location. If you are active on LinkedIn and people you meet at networking are too, it can feel like you are in more frequent contact than you are, which can be helpful for staying top of mind.

However, it is also valuable to have a plan for contacts you met that you want to stay in touch with. Deciding who these people will be is often a combination of people you like and business opportunity. You need to have a process and system to make sure you maintain contact and continue to build the relationships you want. Relationships that start at an event can be likened to seeds you plant in the garden – they need soil, water, and air to become fully grown plants. It is the same with relationships. They need some commitment and input to flourish. It might feel like a huge effort, but once you have the skills and it becomes a regular part of your working life, you will see the benefits. If you have business development responsibility, it is essential to build a strong network that will bring you valuable connections and business over time.

Someone may have liked you and could imagine instructing you, but at the point they met you, didn't have a need. Six months later, they or someone they know may have a need for what you offer but if you haven't continued to build the relationship, they are likely to instruct someone else.

Staying top of mind is vital. Some firms have systems to keep track of contacts, which can be helpful in many ways. If this exists in your firm, use it to make notes on people you have met and set reminders to reconnect with them. People really appreciate you remembering things about them so if you don't have a great memory then making some notes can be helpful. Even the process of typing key points is more likely to help it stay in your mind. If you are attending regular events, you may want to review who you met there last time before you attend again.

If your firm doesn't have a system, then setting a diary reminder (also with some notes) is useful. When to get in touch with someone you have met at an event depends on circumstances – I typically think two to three months works well, but if they mentioned something specific in a different time frame then you may want to note that. That may be something personal like a wedding, or professional such as a date when a project is likely to be kicked off. You wouldn't want to reconnect at exactly that point as this can appear over eager but sometime after works well.

Strategic reconnection might just be a check in email, a useful resource you thought would interest them, or a coffee or lunch suggestion. The more you get to know people and build trust, the more likely business opportunities are.

In conclusion
If you work on these skills, a couple at a time to make them new habits, not only will you feel more confident, but you will be more positively memorable

amongst people you meet at events. This is vital as there are a lot of lawyers in the market. Standing out as someone who is clearly knowledgeable but also, importantly, knows how to interact positively and confidently with potential clients and referrers helps them feel reassured you would do a good job for them, if they engaged or referred you. Being top of someone's mind in this way, combined with an ongoing relationship building strategy, is vital to win more business. Few lawyers really focus on the skills they need to develop business from networking so if you do, you are likely to be successful. Networking at events is a highly important business development activity and it does get easier with time and practice.

Chapter 5:
Female-friendly networking – the power of social media

By Belinda Lester, managing director and founder, Lionshead Law

I think that most women would agree that "traditional" networking favors men – rounds of golf, late night drinking, residential conferences, camaraderie, and often behaving quite badly. Men have always found it easy to network as the workplace, and particularly the legal workplace, was designed with the needs of men in mind. Most of the larger City law firms in the UK still, even post-pandemic, retain a "long hours" office-based culture that, let's face it, relies on there being a supportive person (assumed to be a wife) in the background, ensuring that the children are cared for and the home fires kept burning whilst the important work is carried out by the important men.

The majority of law firms, even the smaller ones, still operate in this way, with a return to the office post-pandemic, rather than remote working, being the way that lawyers feel best able to demonstrate their supposed commitment – something that puts women lawyers at an even greater disadvantage. If law firms are now offering hybrid working, and that way of working is mostly taken up by women or men who have already made partner, then arguably this has made matters even more difficult for women than they were before COVID-19. If you add to this the fact that many firms focus their corporate entertaining towards the needs of their mostly male or corporate clients whilst the female lawyers, despite making up over 50 percent of qualifying solicitors, still often find themselves either unable to attend, as spare parts or, even worse, not invited, then women definitely need to find alternative ways to harness their networks and build their own connections.

Networking for women can be hard work but it doesn't have to be. Before starting my own business, I had been a partner in two law firms, specializing in employment law. Although I had made partnership, I had always struggled to build a strong client base or to generate significant fees. The traditional law firm structure and the old fashioned "hourly rate" model just didn't seem to work for employment law – I couldn't meet the right clients and I certainly couldn't sell my services on an hourly rate. Networking events tended to be at times that were simply not workable for me as a working mother or they were marketed as women's networking events and were full of small, often "kitchen table", business owners who had little or no need for legal services or, if they did, certainly couldn't afford my rates. I knew that I was a good lawyer, I knew that the clients I had were very happy with the service I provided, but I also knew that I wasn't a good business developer, despite being a natural communicator. As a mother of two young children, the thought of building up a practice and a client base was not only daunting, it was seemingly impossible. Even with a babysitter, I couldn't face the thought of going out night after night to networking events and speaking to other people who were really only interested in selling their own goods and services rather than listening to me extol the virtues of the firm I worked for and the services I had to offer.

This made leaving the comfort of a stable job and starting my own firm, Lionshead Law, particularly daunting. However, I knew that I had some great ideas for how I could make it both female-friendly *and* successful and, a decade on, I am so glad I backed my instinct and went for it. In the past year the firm has grown rapidly as, with my children now in their late teens, I am able to throw my all into expansion and am proud that I have been able to turn it into the "alternative" virtual law firm that works for everyone (but particularly women) that I dreamt of back in 2013. I knew even then (long before the pandemic made remote working and video calling the norm) that the traditional law firm was a dying beast and that new working models that, happily, were far more suited to the needs of women, were going to be the way forward. So, I took the plunge, leaving my last firm in July 2013, and never looked back.

So what was my dream and what is now the reality? Well, the first decision I took was that Lionshead Law was to have no offices, no hourly rate, and no normal office hours. It was going to offer specialist employment law advice for fixed fees or on a monthly retainer at affordable rates due to the minimal overheads. Our tag line was to be "Always here for you…", which meant that clients would know that advice was available even outside normal business hours. What this would mean for the solicitors (initially just me) would be that they would not be stuck at their desks between 9am and 6pm, Monday to Friday, as there would be no expectation from the clients that they would be. Knowing that they could contact their solicitor any time of day, any day of the week, would mean that they would immediately lose the expectation that he or she would always be sitting at their desk in an office. If their solicitor was on the school run whilst dishing out advice, the client wouldn't care so long as the advice given was sound. This model, in my mind, was going to be great news for the clients, and even better news for the solicitors, especially those with other commitments outside of work. Not having normal working hours did not mean any expectation on my part that solicitors should work around the clock. On the contrary, it was to enable them to work at times best suited to them and their other needs.

So, with my fabulous ideas, I found myself on 2 September 2013, my first day of trading, sitting at my brand new desk with a brand new business and fewer clients than I could count on one hand. I now needed to get out there and generate business. But "getting out there" was something I had never been particularly good at and really didn't want to do. I had to think about what I *was* good at and utilize that instead. I had always been an avid "Facebooker", using it to post the usual kid/holiday photos, keeping in touch with old friends, and occasionally (OK, maybe more than occasionally) venturing into political debate. However, sitting at my desk, trying to work out how best to generate work, I found myself browsing the myriad Facebook groups. There are groups on Facebook for everything you can think of, and these groups are populated by thousands of people – thousands of people who are interested in the same thing, all together in one place, and a place I could access without leaving the comfort of my own home! This was my lightbulb moment.

As I sat there thinking about my business, I tried to work out who my perfect clients would be and how I could target them from home. At first, I thought I needed to focus solely on companies as they would go on retainer and provide a constant income stream. However, I then thought about how to best get free advertising, given I needed to grow the business without any external financial investment. It seemed obvious to me that doing a great job for a client and getting referred by them to someone else was the way to go, especially with no advertising or marketing budget to speak of. That's when it dawned on me that my focus needed to be on growing my claimant practice and not, as I had originally thought, my respondent one. A happy individual is far more likely to recommend their solicitor to someone else than a happy corporate. So, whilst for employment lawyers, most people we meet are potential clients – as most people are either employers or employed – I could see that targeting and doing good work for employees (potential claimants) was likely to generate a bigger personal profile, leading to a bigger brand profile, which would then lead me to being able to better target businesses who would then go on retainer. I didn't think that claimants would, themselves, generate much in the way of fees but I was entirely wrong on that count and, in fact, focusing my business development strategy towards the individual rather than the corporate has turned out to be extremely successful and lucrative – again because of the extremely flexible way in which the firm operates, which ensures lower overheads and therefore greater flexibility on fees.

Whilst in the UK all employees with more than two years' service can bring unfair dismissal claims, the only ones who can bring claims with uncapped damages and with less than two years' service are those whose dismissals are deemed "automatically unfair", or those who have suffered unlawful discrimination. Which group probably suffers most often from discrimination in the workplace? You guessed it – women – and particularly working mothers or women who have just had a baby. So, with that in mind, I joined as many Facebook groups as I could that I knew would be mostly populated by working mothers. What I didn't do (and in fact, what you're not normally allowed to do in Facebook groups) is go in there and advertise myself. Direct selling rarely works in person and it certainly doesn't work on Facebook. What Facebook does is enable people to interact with like-minded people, offering support and guidance, building rapport and trust. That is what I set out to do in the groups I joined, and it is what led me to realize what an incredible marketing tool Facebook can be. In subsequent years, I came to understand how important other social networks are in helping women make connections without leaving the comfort of their homes.

Facebook groups
There are Facebook groups for pretty much anything you can think of. Initially setting up as a sole practitioner, I actively searched for groups that would likely have disgruntled employees in it, and I quickly discovered a group called "Flexible Working for Mums Like Me". The group was started by a fantastic working mum called Katy Fridman who has herself, utilizing the power of social media, now turned it into "Flexible Working People" as part of a fantastic and thriving recruitment business for people looking for flexible jobs. As anticipated, the group was full of women encountering difficulties in the workplace and I was able to answer their questions without giving any hard sell. This frequently led to formal instructions. However, all Facebook groups and particularly those that attract women (and a great many active Facebook users are women) often contain people who are seeking advice and, frequently, legal advice relating to their jobs, their divorces, their neighbor

disputes, conveyancing, or the setting up of their own businesses. So, these groups are ideal networking spaces for female lawyers. Women will either ask a question to the group or, quite often, they will ask if anyone in the group can recommend a solicitor. If you become active in the groups, joining in discussions and answering questions (but stressing that your response ought not be relied upon as it is general rather than specific), you will find that, in a relatively short space of time, you become the solicitor that other members of the group recommend. You will also find that offering a bit of free advice in a forum will frequently result in a direct message, which will then lead to a paid instruction. This is exactly what happened for me, and it continues to be an incredible source of business.

Not only that, it has enabled me to do "offline" networking in a more focused and targeted way. Facebook and other online platforms enable you to filter the people you would like to meet first. Only once you have built up a relationship online with someone with whom you believe you have business synergy do you set up a face-to-face meeting. Don't underestimate the importance of that. It's all too easy to stay online and think that you never actually have to do any real-life networking again, but there is no substitute for looking someone in the eye and getting a feel for them.

But Facebook isn't the only social network out there. Whilst I believe it is the best for female solicitors, especially those working in the fields of employment, family, private client, and other "people centered" areas of law, it is important to build your brand and your firm's brand across all relevant social networks, as that will ensure you come up more often in Google searches. It will also enable you to develop a cohesive brand identity. Other social networks, although not necessarily great on their own, if utilized cleverly and correctly alongside Facebook, can certainly help you to develop your network further.

LinkedIn

When I started the firm, I focused my online networking heavily on Facebook as that was my gateway to the types of clients I wanted to attract. I was skeptical about LinkedIn. I saw it as a really dry, self-promoting version of Facebook for business and I didn't fully appreciate how powerful a tool it is for profile raising. LinkedIn is the business person's Facebook and, like Facebook, it has groups and forums where you can contribute, post articles, and generally make a noise to get yourself noticed. By following hashtags you can find posts on relevant subject areas, which you can then comment on, thereby establishing yourself as an expert in your field. This, again, can be an excellent way to raise your profile in a business arena and may prove more fruitful than Facebook if it is senior management or business owners you are looking to target, or even individuals. It's all about name recognition. However, on LinkedIn, it's important to remember that everyone is selling themselves for work. On Facebook, this generally isn't the case, so, as a female lawyer, you are already at a significant advantage.

Admittedly, until recently, I was something of a LinkedIn sceptic. I knew it served a purpose but I wasn't entirely sold. That all changed when I decided to accelerate the growth of the firm. In order to grow, I needed to find more lawyers as Lionshead Law is a consultancy-based firm and more lawyers generating income obviously increases profitability. However, as the firm doesn't have employees, traditional recruitment strategies don't work. I needed to find a way of attracting solicitors away from the safety of employment and into the relative insecurity (but potentially significantly more lucrative) of consultancy. LinkedIn is where all the lawyers are to be found in one place, so it's a great way to become known amongst your peers. That applies equally to the usual business development. Comment on other solicitors' posts, and keep your name and the type of work you do prominent. That way you can build your legal network, which increases the chances of a lawyer in a different practice area or with a conflict passing work on to you. It also means that those who are interested in the topics being discussed will see you and not just the original poster.

X (formerly known as Twitter)
Then there's X (formerly known as Twitter). For this to be really effective, you need to ensure you know how to use hashtags, thereby ensuring you get a targeted readership for your posts, as only then will you generate followers and a brand identity. When I post, I often use the hashtag #ukemplaw as that hashtag is followed by a large number of people in my field – especially my target audience of HR professionals. Some people love X and it is true that, if you are able to generate a significant following, you can establish yourself as an expert. However, I would say that, unless you have something pithy and interesting to say at least once a day, and unless you can ensure huge numbers of relevant people are going to read your posts, it's probably not going to be your best friend in terms of business development and networking. Posting something interesting or engaging with other users is pretty time-consuming.

Having said all that, X can be great for making other contacts. Journalists often use the hashtag #journorequest when they want contributors for an article or a TV or radio show. Look out for these hashtags as, if it's something you're an expert on, you could find yourself on television within 24 hours – which has happened to me!

Instagram/Threads
Finally, Instagram and its new X-like Threads. Amazingly, Instagram can be a very good way to support the brand (whether personal or corporate) that you are developing on other social media. Illustrating legal points with pictures, to which text can be added (both under the photo and separately on Threads), provides further interest and has the advantage of also being easily shared on Facebook.

For women, social media is a Godsend. To my mind, it has been the most important tool for levelling the business development playing field for women. Women are avid users, women are actively engaged in forums, and female lawyers have unique access to those women – arguably in a way that, for once, the men don't! Go out there and social network – or should I say, stay in!

Chapter 6:
Overcoming blocks around self-promotion

By Susan Heaton-Wright, founder, Superstar Communicator

A key characteristic of successful people is that they take credit for their contribution. They have control over their career and ensure others know their successes. The challenge for many women is that, culturally, they are brought up not to self-promote, which negatively impacts their career prospects. But they are also uncomfortable accepting compliments or positive feedback.

Imagine a popstar not accepting applause after a brilliant performance. Instead of taking a curtain call, she disappears. She doesn't acknowledge the audience and doesn't return onstage to accept their approval. She manages to escape the theatre without her fans seeing her. Instead of engaging with people waiting at the stage door, she has instructed everyone to leave.

How would you feel if a sportsperson ignored the applause when they won? Or even worse, instructed everyone to be silent following their success, and didn't acknowledge the fans who were bewildered by this.

You would be annoyed, disappointed, and – if you thought more about it – would consider this rude, arrogant, and unacceptable behavior. You might question their values, their ego, and would probably feel short-changed.

If I can contrast this with a positive experience with the late Jessye Norman – the world respected operatic soprano in the 1990s – who I was honored to look after when she came to perform at Symphony Hall Birmingham. Before the performance she didn't allow anyone to speak or engage with her. However, after a long, sensational performance, she sat in the foyer for two-and-a-half hours, where fans met her and had CDs, programs and cards signed by The Diva. I still recollect how fans and members of the audience felt – not only were they thrilled with meeting this extraordinary artiste, they had the opportunity to thank her, compliment her, and share their gratitude.

People often give compliments to express admiration, kindness, or appreciation, so accepting them graciously can foster good feelings and strengthen relationships. If we don't, we risk others remembering this.

So why is it that so many people, particularly women, brush off a compliment when others are expressing their admiration? How often do we receive a compliment, even a small one, and undervalue what is being said to us? In the last week alone, I have heard a number of examples.

"You look lovely in that dress." "Oh, this old thing!"

"Well done for mentioning that point in the meeting." "Oh, was it OK? I thought I was being pushy!"

"I have some good news – I was runner up in this international award." "We need to celebrate this and let your organization know of your success!" "Oh no, I can't possibly do that."

We all do it – especially women!

Take the example of someone complimenting you over a pitch:

"Congratulations; that was a great pitch!"

"Not really; I made loads of mistakes."

I hold my hand up here, since this was my response when a colleague complimented me on the pitch I'd just delivered!

What is happening here:

- You are downplaying yourself and the contribution you are making. You are openly acknowledging, to the world, that you believe your contribution or performance was not of a high quality. Is that good for your career?
- It makes the compliment-giver feel bad. They don't have to compliment – they are being generous – yet you have undermined their generous comment.
- It is questioning their opinion. This is the most important point – they have a perspective on how a performance, appearance, or contribution is. You are openly challenging their judgement. Is that a good career move, especially if this is a more senior colleague?
- You are telling the person they do not know how to appreciate real achievement. If they have complimented you on your presentation skills and they also present, you are telling them they are a failure so they may go away from giving you the compliment feeling worse about themselves. Surely we don't want this?

Have you ever noticed a tendency in yourself or others to feel uncomfortable in receiving a compliment?

This can play out in different ways:

- *Assumed criticism.* Someone tells you, "You look great", and rather than

receiving this as appreciation you think, "They must usually think I look terrible".
- *Deflecting and denying.* You're told, "That was a delicious meal", and you reply, "Oh, it needed more salt". You are told, "I love what you're wearing", and you reply, "What, this old thing?".
- *Ping-pong deflection/denying.* You're told, "I liked what you said in the team meeting today", to which you reply, "It was nothing, I thought you made some really good points though". Or "You're looking great", to which you reply, "I need to tone up, but you look really good".
- *Ping pong compliments.* You're told, "You're looking good today", to which you reply "So are you, you look great".

Why do we do this?
- *A fear of appearing big-headed or arrogant.* This can be deep rooted in childhood and cultural conditioning, with parents, school, and religions telling us not to think we are special. This is especially true of women and girls. I was certainly told, "Don't get too big for your boots" as a child.
- *Doubting the unconditional nature of the compliment.* In this instance, we feel compelled to return the compliment out of a fear that the compliment was not freely given but was conditional. We worry we will let down the other person if we do not keep to the agreement for mutual praise. This might have been the pattern of behavior as a child, which we repeat as an adult.
- *Low self-esteem.* This results in us believing we do not deserve the compliment. Or we dislike having the spotlight put on us, so we push it away. In our minds, we question why they gave the compliment, and whether there was an underlying motive because it couldn't possibly be true.
- *Fear of being seen to be proud or arrogant.* This might come from a belief that it is more honest to deny a compliment, or early conditioning that told us not to think of ourselves as special or better than others. We might have been admonished if we showed signs of "pride", which may just have been healthy self-esteem.
- *Being a perfectionist.* In your own mind, nothing you do can ever be good enough, despite someone taking the time to compliment you.
- *Negative self-view.* You feel you see your own faults and failings better than the other so cannot accept their praise. You feel they do not really

know your true limitations and, if they did, they would not offer the compliment.

Of course it's not fundamentally wrong to not accept a compliment, but it can be a missed opportunity to connect positively with someone. The compliment giver is being generous – they don't have to say anything, but they have. If you brush off compliments or refuse to accept them, it might come across as dismissive or unappreciative, which can inadvertently hurt the person who gave the compliment. As well as minimizing the way you contribute to a case or project in your firm, there is a possibility they won't bother to compliment you in the future.

This is important: it is OK to accept compliments and recognition that you contributed to a case or project.

So, how do you accept a compliment?

- Recognise that people are taking a risk in saying what they appreciate about you and are putting themselves out by saying something they have seen in you they like. Connect with a feeling of gratitude and respect for them as you hear the compliment.
- Accept the compliment. Take a deep breath, smile and say, "Thank you".
- Praise the compliment. You may wish to acknowledge the appreciation by saying something in praise of the compliment, such as, "Thank you, that means a lot to me to hear that", or "Thank you, that's kind of you to say that".
- Practice – in the safety of your personal life. Get used to accepting a compliment and start enjoying the experience.

If we are reluctant to accept compliments from others, there are also messages that if we share good news, we could be perceived as bragging. We therefore won't take the credit for our contribution or let others know about our successes.

The bias against women boasting about their successes – or even the perception you are bragging by association in accepting a compliment – is rooted in societal norms, stereotypes, and expectations regarding gender roles and behavior. This bias can be attributed to several factors:

1. *Social expectations*. There is a societal expectation that women should be modest, humble, and self-effacing. When women openly talk about their accomplishments or skills, they may be perceived as violating these expectations, leading to negative judgments or backlash.

2. *Double standards*. Women often face double standards regarding self-promotion. While men are often praised or seen as confident when they talk about their achievements, women may be labelled as arrogant, boastful, or aggressive for exhibiting similar behavior. This is still relevant today and could negatively impact your professional brand.
3. *Cultural norms*. Cultural norms and traditions in many societies reinforce the idea that women should prioritize others' needs and accomplishments over their own. This can create a stigma around self-promotion for women, as it may be viewed as selfish or inappropriate.
4. *Perceived threat*. Some individuals may perceive confident and assertive women as threatening or challenging traditional power dynamics. This perception can contribute to a bias against women who openly celebrate their successes. I should add that many women perceive other women who self-promote negatively too – it is not exclusively men who perceive confident women in this way.

Here's an example that illustrates how both men and women may exhibit bias against a woman celebrating her success.

Imagine a workplace scenario where a woman, let's call her Lisa, has just received recognition for a successful project she led. Lisa decides to share the news with her colleagues during a team meeting. Here's how different individuals might react:

1. *Male colleague response:* One of Lisa's male colleagues, David, responds by congratulating her and acknowledging her hard work. However, David's tone and body language convey a subtle hint of surprise, as if he didn't expect Lisa to achieve such success. This reaction stems from his unconscious biases about women's capabilities in leadership roles, leading David to be somewhat skeptical or dismissive despite offering congratulations. His non-verbal communication didn't match what he said, highlighting the mixed messages.
2. *Female colleague response:* Another colleague, Heather, who is a woman, reacts differently. While Heather verbally congratulates Lisa, she also makes a comment like, "Wow, Lisa, you're really showing everyone what you're capable of!" This comment, although seemingly positive, carries a hint of reservation, slight patronization, or discomfort. Heather's response reflects her internalized biases about women's behavior and the expectation that women should be more modest and

reserved about their achievements. There could also be an element of jealousy surrounding Lisa's success.

In both cases, there's a subtle form of bias against Lisa celebrating her success. David's reaction reflects skepticism or surprise based on gender stereotypes about women's competence, while Heather's response suggests a discomfort with overt self-promotion by women. These reactions highlight the challenges women often face in navigating societal expectations and biases when it comes to celebrating their accomplishments.

A 2021 study[1] showed that 82 percent of participants hide a success from a loved one, coworker, or stranger, often out of a desire to avoid bragging. Only last week I shared some good news to my mother who is a widow – I thought the good news would be a boost and of interest to her. However, the subtle messages were that I was bragging and that it was a one-off. I am able to see this dynamic working, but it was a shame that my mother (who was possibly doing this subconsciously) responded in this way. I am sure readers here will have experienced similar situations and are therefore reluctant to share good news elsewhere, or have a deep rooted belief that it is somehow wrong to share a success.

The challenge is that if you don't self-promote or take the credit for your work, others will not recognize the contribution you are making. This could impact on your promotion prospects and how you are valued within the competitive legal sector.

Remembering to acknowledge successes

So why am I discussing this in a business development book?

There are some ways you can feel more comfortable about taking the credit for your work and promoting yourself.

One exercise is an adapted version of the "Three Good Things"[2] exercise created by Professor Martin Seligman.

I have adapted the original exercise to focus not just on three points that made you happy but for you to get used to acknowledging your contribution and how it made you feel.

At the end of your working day, spend five minutes reflecting and writing down answers to the following questions.

1. Write down three things that went well today. This might be something as simple as sharing your opinion in a meeting, having an excellent meeting with a client, or even completing a task.

2. Reflect on how it made you feel. This is an opportunity for you to personally be proud of what you have achieved.
3. What contribution did you make? I want you to "own" what you contributed. This is a safe place to be assertive and delighted with your contribution.

In the original "Three good things" exercise, it was recommended you do this for seven days. However, I recommend you complete the exercise for 30 days, to embed the positive habit of taking ownership and being satisfied with your achievements. You are creating new positive habits of how you perceive your contribution.

As Professor Seligman said:

"A sense of accomplishment is a result of working toward and reaching goals, mastering an endeavour, and having self-motivation to finish what you set out to do. This contributes to wellbeing because individuals can look at their lives with a sense of pride."[3]

Remember – celebrating our achievements can boost our self-confidence and motivate us to achieve more.[4] This is a powerful yet easy way to give yourself permission to let others know what your contribution is and what your successes have been.

Another excellent way for you to be comfortable sharing your success or contribution is to have facts or data to back up your success.

I recently read the following quote from Simone Biles:

"I've won five world titles and if I say, 'I'm the best gymnast there is,' [the reaction is] 'Oh, she's cocky. Look at her now.' No, the facts are literally on the paper."[5]

This is THE Simone Biles, saying she's worried others will perceive her as being cocky. THE Simone Biles, who is the best female gymnast EVER. However, the invaluable part of the quote is that she knows her personal beliefs of being the best gymnast there is, are based on fact. There is no arguing against her achievements.

Based on this, how could you add proof to your confidence or success? Could it be sharing income you have generated for the firm or chambers? Your success rate of winning cases? Feedback or testimonials from clients?

Start building a library of data proof to back up your achievements. This makes it easier for you to self-promote. If there is any pushback, you have the evidence to support you.

The power of dual promotion
Another technique for self-promotion is to combine it with other promotion activities – such as complimenting or giving credit to others whilst self-promoting. This is often called "dual-promotion". Individuals are able to project warmth and capability to make more favorable impressions to colleagues and clients than they do by only self-promoting.[6]

The only point to be aware of is that you don't fall into the trap of promoting others – giving them all the credit and ignoring your contribution. Of course, you will come across as a generous person, but it is so important to let others know of your own contribution and abilities too.

Another trap we could potentially fall into is being determined to share our successes but not being interested in anyone else's accomplishments. In 2020, just before the pandemic, I was honored to be invited to the House of Lords along with 99 other extremely successful women as part of the F:Entrepreneur 100 Best Female Entrepreneurs of 2020. Every single woman there was truly remarkable and I loved hearing what they were doing. I was also able to share my achievements with everyone but one woman. She dominated the conversation, sharing her successes but having no interest in anyone else's. In fact, she walked away or talked over other women when they started to share their achievements. I still remember her arrogance and rudeness because she made the conversation all about her, no one else.

Building a library of case studies
This is useful when considering interviews and appraisals – examples to share with clients and during networking opportunities. Building a library of successes, case studies, and very short stories to share is a powerful tool for you to develop. This demonstrates your value and credibility and shows that you are capable of doing the job. For a number of years, I have kept and recorded positive feedback, reviews, and testimonials to add value to any work I do. If I need to share examples of my work or have proof and validation from other people, it is readily available to share.

I recommend you build your own library of case studies. As part of your professional development, consider projects and cases you have been involved in. These could include specific cases, projects, and tasks you have worked on, meetings with clients and prospects, and work/income that you have won. Write short case studies. Keep a library of these.

How to structure your case studies or stories

The key to these case studies or stories are that they are brief and to the point. Interview coaches will recommend you share case studies with the "STAR" structure:

1. *Situation*. Describe the situation and when it took place. You are setting the scene for your case study.
2. *Task*. Explain the task and the challenge articulately.
3. *Action*. Provide details about the action you took to solve the challenge. Avoid going into too much detail.
4. *Result*. Conclude with the result of your action and ensure you acknowledge your contribution to the case study.

An example might be:

1. *Situation*. We had a client who wanted to evict a non-paying tenant.
2. *Task*. The client was owed a significant sum and wanted repossession of the property.
3. *Action*. We advised the client and produced the paperwork to evict the client.
4. *Result*. Because of this, the landlord regained possession of the property to sell.

You will notice that I have not gone into significant detail; the comments at all stages are what I refer to as "headlines", providing a clear indication of the case study. Avoid going into too much detail and going off topic. If the person wants more information, they will ask you.

It is essential for you to take ownership of your contribution to the case study or story. This is not the time for false modesty where "my team" completed this.

Where could you use these?

- Appraisals. It is essential to prepare for any appraisal to ensure you make the most of this opportunity. This is a genuine chance for you to demonstrate what you have achieved and how you have reached any goals set for your professional development. It's also a chance for you to state what your future career goals are. Before the appraisal, reflect on what you have achieved since the last appraisal.

- Have you met any specific targets or career development goals?
- How could you demonstrate what you have achieved? Remember, this is a professional conversation between you and a more senior member of your firm.
- What have you learnt? Have you increased your skill set? If so, let your line manager know this. You could use some of your case studies to show this.
- Consider five or six case studies to use to demonstrate your value.
- Your manager will discuss progress and share information with the senior leadership team to recommend talent to be considered for promotion.

This technique is particularly useful for when you are negotiating a promotion or salary raise. However, your success will reflect well on your manager too. Letting him or her know what you have achieved will provide stories or proof of how well they are leading their department.

- *As part of your business case for promotion*. Use these in all conversations with colleagues – and especially people from other departments and senior people. There are occasions where you will meet a colleague or senior person in the office, or you might attend an event with someone from your firm. When they ask, "How are things going?" or "What are you working on now?", share at least one case study.
- *Networking*. Have a current project (subject to privacy) or a recent project (again, subject to privacy) where you can demonstrate your value. When someone asks what you are doing, say this is a case I have been working and, in those four sentences, you increase your value.
- *Clients*. It is likely you will be invited to client events. This is a perfect time to remind them what good work you deliver. Without breaking any confidentiality, you could share a case study that could be relevant to their sector or current challenges.
- *Prospecting*. When you have meetings with potential clients, curating case studies of similar challenges both demonstrates your credibility and ability to support them but also reassures them that you are the right person to be instructed.
- *Networking internally*. We often forget that anyone we engage with internally is building our network. There are going to be colleagues who influence decisions.
- *Building your business case for progressing for promotion*. As well as

collecting information on the clients you are working with and new business you have personally brought in, ensure you have a few case studies to simply illustrate the quality of work you have accomplished. Your senior colleagues will ask further questions, but these initial case studies will provoke interest and curiosity in your work.

What else should we do to be comfortable taking the credit and self-promoting?

I have mentioned before that I have kept my own case studies and "Success Journal". I keep testimonials and positive feedback I have received from clients, colleagues, and customers. I use some of these as "data" and credible proof of my achievements. I would recommend you do this, alongside your case study library.

Why it is important for women to take the credit and self-promote?

An article featured in *Harvard Business Review* titled "Research: How Women Can Build High-Status Networks"[7] tracked 42 global pharmaceutical companies, including thousands of male and females over 25 years to see their career progression.

The study found that, in face-to-face situations with a senior leader, men were more articulate, assertive, and confident. They were comfortable interjecting and interrupting the senior leader. Women were well researched and their conclusions impeccable, but the leaders considered the men to have more potential (based on their own biases) and they would be more likely to be remembered in future when considering future talent. This is, of course, a disadvantage for women who, if they behaved like their male colleagues, may be considered pushy or brash.

Based on this study and my own observations, it is important for senior leadership – as well as ourselves – to recognize existing biases, and it is essential to normalize self-promotion for women. Women should be respected for being assertive and confident, and as more women progress to more senior roles, normalizing this behavior within your firm's women's network is crucial.

I have an idea for celebrating success and practicing self-promotion within your network. This is a skill that, as women, we should be comfortable exercising. I have worked with women's networks in law firms where we set up a time within any meeting to encourage members to share their successes and celebrate together.

- In small groups, share your achievmnets and acknowledge each other. Support each other to be comfortable contributing to the discussion. Ensure there are mixed levels in the groups – more senior women could be role models on how to share a success but also benefit from hearing more junior women's successes, which they could share with their colleagues.
- Allocate a time in any meeting for individuals to share their successes. A suggestion would be for a certain number of members to share their "success case study" to the rest of the group to practice self promotion and taking credit.
- Create a culture in which women celebrate each other's successes, giving permission that it is good for women to self promote.

This chapter has covered why it is important to accept praise and compliments, and why it is important to take the credit for your achievements and ways you could feel more comfortable sharing your successes without coming across as bragging. I have shared research that shows that men are more comfortable doing this and it could be a reason why men progress faster to more senior roles.

Senior leadership and those influencing career progression should be aware of biases against women sharing their achievements. We, as women, could use some of the suggestions I have made to build confidence in self-promoting and to be empowered to do this.

Please feel free to contact me with your successes.

References

1. Roberts, A. R., Levine, E. E., and Sezer, O. (2021). Hiding success. *Journal of Personality and Social Psychology*, 120(5), 1261-1286. https://doi.org/10.1037/pspi0000322.
2. https://ppc.sas.upenn.edu/our-mission
3. Seligman, M. E. (2012). *Flourish: A visionary new understanding of happiness and well-being*. Atria.
4. www.psychologytoday.com/us/blog/1-2-3-adhd/202111/why-its-important-celebrate-small-successes
5. https://ftw.usatoday.com/2019/10/watch-simone-biles-says-shes-the-greatest-gymnast-its-not-out-of-cockiness
6. *Journal of Personality and Social Psychology*. Eric VanEpps Vanderbilt University
7. https://hbr.org/2024/03/research-how-women-can-build-high-status-networks

Chapter 7:
Utilizing AI for strategic advantage in solo and small female-run firms

By Nika Kabiri, JD PhD, Kabiri Consulting

The legal profession is evolving more rapidly than ever, with female-run small and solo firms facing unique challenges as they try to stay competitive. In most cases, surviving and thriving as a practice means being tech-forward. Smaller firms often don't have the resources to hire staff when support is needed, so software for scheduling, accounting, legal research, and practice management may be essential. It's not surprising, then, that many female lawyers are wondering how Artificial Intelligence (AI) might give them an advantage in their small and solo practices.

For many firms, implementing AI-powered solutions seems an obvious strategic move. AI can reduce time spent on tedious tasks while tremendously improving the quality of information-gathering and analysis. Most importantly, AI can improve decision-making by making it better informed and less biased. Because of these obvious benefits, many firms are leveraging AI without much hesitation.

But AI is a tool, not a cure-all, and like all tools, it is most useful when it solves problems it is suited to solve. AI, at its best, is a tool for improving *decision-making*. Where decisions in a firm should be routinized, AI can introduce tremendous efficiencies, leaving lawyers, paralegals, and administrators with time and energy for tasks that require more complex thinking. Where decisions are complex, AI can ensure they are appropriately informed. In short, employing AI just because everyone else is, and in ways other firms are using it, may result in unnecessary risk, if not wasted time and money. Using it strategically, in an effort to improve how choices in your practice are made, makes the most sense.

This chapter explores how AI can be a game-changer for the business side of female-run small and solo practices. It addresses the ways in which AI can streamline processes and minimize biased decision-making, so lawyers can best determine whether and how to incorporate AI in their practices. This chapter also addresses potential drawbacks and ethical considerations that need to be considered before utilizing AI in any firm. By the end of this chapter, you will have a clearer understanding of how AI can enhance your firm's strengths, reduce risks, and propel your practice into a future of unprecedented opportunities for small firm success.

What is AI?
Artificial Intelligence (AI) has swiftly emerged as a cornerstone of innovation in the legal industry. It's therefore necessary that lawyers understand what it is, and more specifically, what it can and cannot do.

Simply put, AI involves computing systems that can perform tasks that humans have exclusively been able to perform, like understanding human language, reasoning, learning, and adapting, and making decisions. As of the publication of this chapter, AI has yet to be able to do all of these things at once.

The AI you are familiar with today is referred to as Artificial Narrow Intelligence (ANI, or Narrow AI). If you've ever interacted with an automated customer support chatbot, you've engaged with Narrow AI. It is used to help diagnose cancer, predict the weather, and so on – but each Narrow AI tool is designed to do only a single thing. For example, Narrow AI that runs a chatbot cannot also analyze weather patterns or predict the probability of cancer (much less plot the overthrow of humanity).

Natural Language Processing (NLP) models are a subset of Narrow AI. They specifically focus on processing and generating human language. If you've ever used ChatGPT, you've used a type of NLP called a Large Language Model (LLM). NLPs can also help with document processing like reading the text in a PDF or generating context-aware responses in online chatbots.

In the future, it is possible that we will see the emergence of AI that can perform multiple tasks, or even AI that is self-aware with consciousness, awareness, and emotions. But for now, considering the benefits and risks of Narrow AI is most useful for lawyers who are incorporating AI into their practice.

When to leverage AI
In the competitive realm of legal services, AI can significantly help female-run small and solo practices level up their business health. But too many firms dive headfirst into AI solutions without asking why they need AI, or whether using it will significantly improve what they're doing. Too many follow the bandwagon and implement AI only because they see other firms doing it. Some use AI because they don't want to appear outdated to clients or the public. Others use AI because they fear that they'll fall behind

competitors if they don't. And some are convinced to use AI by "AI experts" whose livelihoods depend on converting clients to AI fans.

But AI isn't a cure-all. It is simply one tool among many that a business can use to survive and thrive. It is a compelling and powerful tool, but like all tools, if it isn't suited to a specific problem, then it isn't useful. To think properly about the value of AI to your firm, it makes sense to start with the problem you're trying to solve. That way you can identify the right tool for solving it, and know for sure whether AI is the right solution.

AI does best when it solves for four key problems – scarcity, scalability, inefficiency, and risk in decision-making. Let's take each in turn.

When firms cannot hire human resources to perform necessary tasks, they have a scarcity problem. Many small law firms experience the challenge of having more work than they can handle but not enough budget to hire help. Work loads can also ebb and flow, making it difficult to justify hiring full-time staff support. While hiring temporary human help is an option, it's not always feasible – training someone to work temporarily can actually sap resources from a firm. These are circumstances where human resources inside your firm are scarce and AI can step in to help. While AI cannot do everything lawyers, paralegals, or staff support can do, it can perform more mundane or routine tasks that take up time, leaving more bandwidth for you and your team to do more involved work.

When firms can perform tasks well but are unable to perform more of the same tasks for more clients, they have a scalability problem. Many firms function perfectly well with the human resources they have. But if they want to grow, they need to be able to do more with what they have – at least until they grow enough to warrant hiring more human support. One way to do more is to streamline processes to introduce efficiencies. AI can summarize documents, respond to emails, schedule appointments, and perform other tasks at a larger scale than humans.

When too many tasks are tedious, taking more time than seems necessary, firms have an inefficiency problem. Inefficiencies can cripple any business, regardless of whether they want to scale. Many legal professionals can quickly describe the psychological and even emotional annoyance inefficiencies have on them. For example, some legal professionals may find it fatiguing to stop their billable work to respond to an email, schedule an appointment, or search endlessly for a document that should only take seconds to find. AI can not only reduce inefficiencies for the sake of scarcity and scalability – it can alleviate much personal frustration as well.

Finally, when key decisions are rushed they can be poorly informed, and poorly informed decisions can be risky. Much of legal practice involves making critical and often strategic decisions. The outcome of your cases can hinge on the quality of these decisions. But the human brain has limitations – it can only hold and process so much information. It cannot alone conduct sophisticated analyses of data. AI can help ensure that legal practitioners have all the right information in front of them to make the choices they need to make, whether this information comes from AI-powered business analytics, document summarization, or something else.

Many firms have at least one of these four challenges, but not all do. It's important to know whether the success and/or growth of your firm is being compromised by one or more of these four challenges. If it isn't, AI may still be appealing, but incorporating it into your practice may not be a top priority.

How to know what AI tools to use

Many small businesses start inquiring about AI by asking, "What can it do for me?" Or "What AI tools can I choose from?" A better place to start is to ask where in your firm you're experiencing scarcity, scalability challenges, inefficiencies, or risks in choice-making. In other words, perform an audit of your operations and decision-making processes (good consultants with a decision science background can also perform this audit for you).

Once you've identified areas for improvement, next ask: "Is AI, in a general sense, the best solution?" Often, simply implementing different human processes, without AI, can solve whatever challenges your firm might face. For example, many businesses, before and after AI, have improved their processes by setting SMART (specific, measurable, achievable, relevant, and time-bound) goals or establishing clear team roles. Simply investing in employee development and training can often solve many efficiency-related problems. So, before rushing to implement AI, consider the trade-offs.

Once you've decided that AI is in fact what your firm needs, you can start exploring tools that specifically address the challenges you are facing. But just because a tool exists, and others are using it, doesn't mean that tool is right for your firm. A major error many businesses make is in adopting an AI tool simply because everyone else in the industry is doing so. This type of decision is an example of bandwagon bias. Instead, consider what your firm's specific needs are, and find an AI tool that's relevant to those. Keep in mind that what matters is solving for scarcity, scalability, inefficiency, and risk, and not doing what's popular.

For example, one of the most direct applications of AI in legal practice is the use of AI-powered chatbots for enhanced client communication. These chatbots simulate conversation with potential and existing clients, responding near-instantaneously to standard inquiries, freeing lawyers and support staff from managing this type of routinized task. AI-powered chatbots can handle initial consultations, gather basic information, and answer frequently asked questions, ensuring that clients receive immediate attention. Aside from scaling client communications, AI can sift through vast legal databases to find relevant case law, statutes, and legal precedents in a fraction of the time it would take a human researcher. However, if scarcity or scalability aren't core challenges in a practice, using AI for client communications or legal research may not be necessary.

AI-powered tools can also significantly reduce time and energy spent on repetitive administrative tasks. AI can help with document automation and management, relying on databases of templates to create legal documents so that lawyers don't need to repeatedly recreate such documents from scratch. AI systems can also quickly analyze and sort through documents, including contracts, identifying key clauses, potential issues, and modifications, saving practices hours of time in manual review. AI-powered scheduling tools can help manage appointments and court dates, reducing the likelihood of conflicts and time spent managing calendars.

However, if processes are already in place to handle these repetitive tasks – at scale and with minimal error – then using AI may not be needed.

AI can also empower informed decision-making. In addition to providing suggested improvements to contracts and other documents, AI analytics can offer business insights valuable to female-run practices. It can analyze market trends by using social trends data to predict which services might be in highest demand. It can conduct competitive analyses to understand the strengths and weaknesses of competing firms. It can analyze client feedback to determine how to improve the client experience.

However, if no decisions need to be made around gaining a competitive business advantage, using AI for these purposes may not be worthwhile.

As a tool, AI can solve many types of problems within a practice. And given that AI is evolving at a rapid pace, its benefits could multiply quickly. It is therefore important for all legal practitioners to stay informed about how AI is developing and how it's being used in the legal profession.

One way to stay informed is to read articles about AI from individuals who are known experts in AI and AI governance and compliance. One way to learn who these are is to pay attention to who is being quoted in the media. Of course, many experts do not get media attention, but this is a good place to start. You can also look online for academics who teach AI or machine learning at university level, and see if they have a blog. These days, websites like Substack can be great places to find AI experts sharing their points of view.

But be sure to learn from those who have a legitimate professional history working with machine learning or AI, or who have long immersed themselves in the social, cultural, and ethical issues related to AI. Some self-proclaimed AI experts have not been immersed in the field for very long and may claim to be knowledgable but without the background to support it. Finally, be sure to pay attention to experts with all points of view on AI – not just the naysayers and not just the evangelists.

Ethical considerations

The benefits of AI are significant, but employing AI should not be done without careful forethought. Concerns surrounding AI may, for some legal professionals, outweigh the benefits. On the other hand, if concerns are misplaced, law practices could unwittingly choose against AI tools that could significantly benefit their business.

One primary concern about AI is that it could replace the role of humans. In the legal profession, this could have profound implications for how law is practiced. As AI takes over the functions of case research and document analysis, the roles of "paralegal" and "lawyer" may be redefined. Some argue that some roles in the legal profession may disappear altogether. Proponents of AI argue that AI complements, rather than replaces, what legal professionals do. AI can give legal professionals time and mental energy to perform higher-level tasks such as strategic thinking and client relationship-building. Ultimately, it is important to remember that currently AI cannot itself eliminate jobs or replace workers. It is up to legal practitioners – independently and institutionally – to decide how AI should be used in the profession.

Privacy is another major concern. Legal practices handle vast amounts of sensitive data, so female-run practices must ensure that AI systems comply with all data protection laws. Again, AI itself cannot violate privacy. It is up to the humans who design and use it to ensure that protections are in place. It is also up to legal practitioners and the profession to decide how transparent law practices should be with their clients when using AI-powered tools.

Another criticism of AI surrounds potential bias in its algorithms. If AI systems are "trained" on biased data (if they rely on biased data in performing their tasks), then their output will also be biased. This is particularly concerning in the legal space, where impartiality is essential to ensuring justice. It is therefore important to scrutinize the data that your AI tools are being trained on, to understand its limitations, and to be objective about just how confident one can be in their output.

How can you do this? First of all, make sure you are clear on the data your AI tool is being "trained" on (or, what information, documentation, or numbers your tools are relying on to perform its tasks). For example, ChatGPT data is sourced from a wide variety of sources on the internet, including social media posts and comments. Some of these sources may offer accurate information and others might not. It's no surprise, then, that ChatGPT doesn't always serve up useful information. One alternative is to create your own GPT in a paid OpenAI account. This way, you can be sure that only documents you trust are being used. To learn to do this, you can access various resources on the internet or hire a consultant to help. Whatever you do, be sure to consult with a specialist in AI compliance, governance, and ethics, to ensure that whatever you do is not compromising client confidentiality or inadvertently allowing private data to seep out.

A final concern surrounding AI involves the issue of how transparent lawyers should be regarding their use of AI. If lawyers are using AI to perform case work, or even to help with decision-making, their clients may feel they have a right to know. When law practices should disclose their use of AI is also something lawyers and the profession as a whole need to address.

Conclusion

AI represents a powerful tool for women lawyers seeking to enhance their business development strategies and thrive in the legal industry. But how to use it, or whether to use it at all, requires some consideration. Jumping on the AI bandwagon without understanding its benefits and drawbacks could be a waste of time and resources for any particular law firm. But no less importantly, it could also throw the legal profession into irreversible ethical dilemmas. Nonetheless, AI is here to stay. The more women lawyers understand it and its uses, and the more intentional they are in employing it in their firms, the more likely they may be to stay ahead of the curve and succeed in a rapidly changing environment.

Chapter 8:
Using technology for business development

By Joanne Brook, Lionshead Law

Introduction

When I decided to take a law degree, I never thought I'd be a solicitor. I thought law would be useful to get me into business but that law as an academic subject was fairly dull. In land law easements were anything but easy, equity would unbalance me, I knew beyond reasonable doubt that criminal law was not for me, that there was a remote chance I might ever use it, and contract law just had too many words! Then I discovered intellectual property law and my heart soared. Something I could finally relate to. Trademarks, brand names, disputed designs, candid creators, exceptional musicians, arising authors, peevish performers, and interesting innovators – these creatives finally made tutorials interesting. Learning cases was as easy as learning the aisles in the supermarket, the floors of a department store, or the riff of a song.

Let loose as a trainee with clients who invented things, designed things, and made things, I realized that to stay in law, I would have to keep meeting endlessly interesting clients. Luckily, I qualified not long after the Federal Networking Council settled on a unanimous term for networking known as "the internet", linked by using the Transmission Control Protocol/Internet Protocol system, which opened up the world we know today.

My clients remain innovators and developers and though from the start of the internet explosion there have been brilliant females in the field, I found myself in a small number of women who were advisors to technology businesses and who worked in "new media" (yes, that was a thing; yes it was "new"; yes, it is a really old fashioned name). Flash-forward 30 years and women are better represented in STEM businesses than ever before and now make up more than half of the legal profession. So how can brilliant women lawyers develop their business with brilliant clients in the mid-2020s and beyond?

The old adage, *"Do something you enjoy, and you'll never work another day in your life"* is as true for legal work as for any job. It's has been my approach and the enthusiasm I have for the work I do shows in the client engagements I have. This chapter is not just about marketing to women and growing your business through sisterhood – it's intended to highlight how you can find a niche and use technology to leverage your expertise for client pursuit.

Small is beautiful
I am an advocate for "niche" work. Niche practice is generally specializing in a small area of work or having particular expertise within a relatively narrow field. My practice is commercial IP. Within that I mostly advise SMEs and rights owners. The rights they own are usually software and creative content – much of that uses big data and, within creative tech, I have focused for 12 years in working with protecting AR and VR creative output. That has led to being particularly specialized in understanding AI and machine learning and increasingly now, on how AI (and quantum computing), will impact the creative industries. Each of these areas is a niche within a niche. Sometimes the direction of the next niche has been driven by client needs and sometimes purely by an interest I have in the subject matter. Each layer means my knowledge will sync with the needs of a prospective client looking for external legal counsel. The question is how do I identify the clients who need me and how do they find me when they do? I'll address that below.

Using tech to be a successful legal advisor
By far the biggest cohort of professionals employed in law are Generation Zs, who grew up in a world of touch screens and whose first mobile was an iPhone. They represent nearly half of the legal profession and they have an expectation of working anywhere at any time. Generation Alpha is also entering the professional now, many having chosen to avoid the traditional degree route (and being saddled with debt) and join via apprenticeship, but who don't expect a job for life. Being digital natives, they are already equipped with the knowledge that there is a better way of learning and working by using technology across all aspects of their home and professional lives. To Gen Z readers – well done, keep going, and stay in touch because genuinely law is about connections.

Generation X and Millennials make up about 36 percent of those in the legal profession and they came of age well before the internet did. Their first phone was probably a Nokia, and they might remember the days when the firm had a laptop that would be shared and assigned to the person who was going on site to take a client the next day. The "laptop" in question weighed about 7kg and was kept in a leather briefcase that weighed roughly the same. Millennial lawyers are now generally in the third stage of their career, having already reached a senior level in the firm. For Gen X and Millennial readers, the need to develop your business is still there and that's why you have picked up this publication, so hello peer.

But why are generational considerations important in a profession that values drive and mental agility as well as accumulated knowledge? They are important because the way lawyers work is changing dramatically. The week before writing this chapter I was at a large legal tech conference in London and although everyone was marveling at the tech on offer, I didn't see anything new there, which tells me change has already happened but the real use cases have not been effected yet and that the profession is on the verge of being disrupted.

If you had to do a quick SWOT analysis on legal services in the medium-term, I suggest it would look something like this:
- *Strengths* – expertise, committed workforce, combined experience of practice, trust in professional advice.
- *Weaknesses* – lack of forward movement in adoption of technology, complacency about change, cost escalation, lack of appeal to users, lack of trust in individual lawyers, lack of access, perceived elitism, increasing cost of indemnity cover for professional practices, ageing workforce with pension needs to cover, inflexible business structure.
- *Opportunities* – a deregulated, decentralized legal services economy, agile access to expert legal services supported by tech, minimal overhead and reduced risk.
- *Threats* – deregulated decentralized legal service provision, entry of automated legal services and non-lawyers to the market, cost erosion, erosion of trust in human lawyers.

Forbes has run a series of pieces in recent years titled "Is AI Coming for Your Job?".[1] For lawyers, the answer is "Yes". AI already does the job of many lawyers really well – always on, mostly accurate, with no hourly rates. AI programs read and write contracts and know case law better than you do. Combining that with data on your clients means AI knows your clients better than you do and is as good at predicting case outcomes as any actuary. This shouldn't come as news and yet the consequences of this revolution and the inevitable outcomes will do for many.

In the medium term (the next three to five years), driven by the demands of clients and changes in access to legal service, supply from non-solicitors and AI-led providers outside of the traditional legal market will march into the legal arena and impact almost every law firm. Who needs legal counsel to interpret a clause when contracts can self-regulate? Why engage a legal team to fight a case when your insurers have used AI to sift through every like contract and predict the likely outcome based on caselaw? Who needs a conveyancer when all land titles are on the blockchain and so are purchaser, vendor, and loan company details? Does a business really need in-house counsel when it can buy in those skills just in time in the territory it needs them in?

Being aware of the reasons for change and what those changes are and are likely to be is vital to know in order to grow and develop your business. The weaknesses and threats in the above "quick-SWOT" outnumber the strengths and opportunities for all lawyers unless they actively engage now. As the threats/opportunities to the profession as we know it come from outside the legal sector, it may seem difficult to predict or identify how to meet the challenges and prepare for them. It is precisely because technology can do so much of the work that lawyers currently do that, we need to adopt it and utilize it to the full extent of our practice and to address the challenges our clients face.

Using tech to secure and develop your work

From chatbots to robots, contract readers, case crunchers, ChatGPT (Law) to more sophisticated Harvey AI, (LUCY, KIRA, and innumerable other acronym names) lawyers are using AI for better legal output for less money and risk.

Whilst the male gender does seem to show prime adoption of technology in use studies (possibly linked to cost, availability, pragmatism of updating/upgrading, sustainability preferences etc.), across devices and technology use, the split is even between men and women. IPSOS[2] recently carried out a study on use of generative AI by 1,000 people, of which the categories of work divided into brainstorming (36 percent), creating visual art (31 percent), and creative writing (30 percent). For those adopting technical use cases such as summarizing documents or subjects or analysing data, the split was 24 percent and 24 percent respectively. The adoption of generative AI for work and creative output is therefore well underway.

Legal practitioners, like everyone else, fall into all or some basic categories of approach and attitude to technology adoption.

- *Trailblazers* have adopted AI and have been implementing tools across

a range of use cases both at work and at home for a couple of years already. They believe that using AI tools will put them ahead of other lawyers and help them achieve their goals with less effort and more efficiency. Trailblazers are often serial adopters of new technology and see something like generative AI as the obvious next step in legal practice and advocate strongly for its use.
- *Investigators* will have started using AI for specific pieces of information, perhaps under a limited type of subscription service. They might use it to research but maintain the value of human interpretation of the output and retain a healthy mistrust of misinformation and bias that they know can creep into AI programs. Investigators might rely too on others to advise whether AI is actually trustworthy, and security is key. Most lawyers will probably fall into this category.
- Law firms that see themselves as *Optimizers* of AI will employ it to take on mundane tasks and reduce legal spend. They might let clients know they are using AI to free-up time for more important "lawyering"!

Knowing the category of practitioner you are, or of the practice you work in, you can plan for how you will both adopt technologies (like AI) into your practice and use it in your work to develop and grow your practice as a whole and how you will be able to use it to identify and develop business development opportunities for client pursuit.

Lawyers wanting to adopt new technologies to maximize business efficiencies and as a tool to attract business have to be in the "trailblazer" or "investigator" categories. For most law firms, investing in bespoke technology is a spectacularly bad idea. First, if you put 20 lawyers in a room you will get 33 different but definitive opinions, which makes it hard to specify the work and avoid scope creep whilst it's being developed. Also, unless you have a practitioner (or better still several) who understands the needs of the business, the reason for the implementation, and the art of the possible within the build and price, the project is likely to overrun on time and cost and fail to deliver according to the 33 opinions.

Firms who have successfully co-developed AI for law have dedicated legal engineers to the project, meaning outputs are likely to be on target, and that they have real "skin in the game" around outcomes. If you want to add a category of expertise to your skillset and have an eye for detail and project management, joining the new brand of legal engineers could add significant value to your CV. Being aware of how these projects work means you can also skill share and coordinate with your clients taking on that role as a new fee-earning avenue, either as an advising solicitor or as a consultant.

To use technology as a tool for business generation and business development, your practice needs to be in the "early majority" to ensure it keeps ahead of technological innovation and can engage with new clients in these sectors as they burgeon. You also must invest in using tech as a "professional consumer" for client advice and communication to avoid being left behind as AI becomes ubiquitous. Being in the "early majority" generally means being in the first third of those likely to adopt the innovation.

According to general Diffusion of Innovation Theory,[3] within about three years of publication of this chapter, it is likely that we will have moved from early adopters into majority adopters and that most legal firms will be using some form of generative technology for research, drafting, client onboarding, client management, document handling, case review, and predictive outcome assessment. The late majority of firms will then either adopt the technology or – through a process of attrition – fail. Using technology to both develop current practice and to secure new work by use of it is essential. As we are in the general phase of early adoption of AI for legal practice, this is the time for that early majority to review the initial success of the Trailblazers and determine that there is still market share and advantage that can be gained in using new technology, before other competitors and other firms offering these services step in, the opportunity is lost, and you then have to play catch up.

Technology can obviously be used to target clients. The data scrapes that can be undertaken by searching the vast encyclopedia of businesses that is Google and of clients that is social media presents enormous opportunities for connecting with clients and identifying and targeting them with tailored messaging. Do be alive to the fact that if your clients are themselves trailblazers, they might baulk at receiving correspondence on paper or as an attachment or being offered more information on a click-through link, which all indicate a thin veneer of adoption of minimal (cheap) tech. To be trailblazing in client attraction and retention, you need to be looking at the new areas of law and readying yourself to become an advisor on them because they are just around the corner. Consider: Practical uses of NFTs for business; how lawyers can use an easy access (low impact) distributed ledger for secure transactions and immutable document retention; circularity law; environmental reparations; how quantum computing will impact on artificial intelligence; issues surrounding ethics of deploying qubits; making the "digital human" – all anticipated for AI by so many science fiction novels and on to multiplanetary universal law "for all mankind".

Emotional intelligence

To succeed in practice, one needs profile, and to gain that, one has to differentiate. It has never been sufficient for a lawyer to claim to be "expert" – that is the most basic expectation our clients can expect. To state that you have X years of experience is increasingly unimportant as new disciplines arise and adaptability and agility are as critical as experience. So how do human lawyers differentiate now to gain profile and business with clients? Where AI can do the job faster, better, cheaper, more accurately, and arguably with more trust, how will human lawyers (as opposed to synthetic ones) differentiate?

I believe that legal practice is primarily a communication business and there are many people with a natural flair for listening and disseminating information who are drawn to law. You only need look at how many lawyers enter broadcasting or publish excellent fiction and artful works of comedy to know that often lawyers have a keen wit and a sense of drama that they no doubt use to great effect in their legal practice. Add to this list of creative endeavors the skills that any woman who has learnt to apply mascara sitting on a bus, email a friend whilst appearing sympathetic on a call to a boyfriend, or feed a child and have a conversation at the same time, and who therefore knows all about multi-tasking, and you have all the requisite skills of the modern lawyer. This ability to assimilate vast amounts of information and retain the nuggets you will need, and to then use them succinctly in a range of scenarios and to engage your clients with good humor, should not be understated. All of these creative skills are particularly useful in the field of technology law, precisely because the subject matter is often nebulous and difficult to explain to those outside of the business. Artificial Intelligence can write like, speak like, appear to "think like" – but it cannot emote like a human. For now, this will remain a point of differentiation and a particular strength of (certain) human lawyers.

As the threat of the digital lawyer and productized legal service provision from non-regulated suppliers rises and crystalizes, the greatest skills a lawyer can deploy to win new business are to listen and to question.

Where I believe women can particularly differentiate and prove that their skill set is as comprehensive and agile, non-linear, and qualitatively comparative as many non-human legal service providers is in the combination of those skills with a natural tendency to share, explain, and resolve matters cooperatively. What may seem like a range of unconnected or left-of-field queries are often the ones that lead to the most productive outcomes. This "multi-lateral" thinking is a positive benefit when working through complicated, interrelated, but not quite applicable laws to find a practical solution to a client's dilemma.

From a scroll with a law inscribed with a quill to AI contract review, use of technology to store, record, and interpret knowledge has always been an imperative for lawyers. As women, we should also use it as part of our professional armory to ensure we remain current and relevant in the ever-changing workplace. The phone we carry in our bags contains more processing power than the computers that built the ISS or NASA's computers that took men to the moon and back. But, a human brain is not just a computer, it does more than process input according to a set of instructions, and (for now) this is its advantage over AI. It thinks, it improves, it creates, and it cares. So long as we see ourselves as the interface between technology and clients, we can grow our businesses by using it intelligently and thoughtfully, recognizing that our clients want us to use technology to improve their experience of legal services and by letting them know we embrace that.

Staying on board and riding the technology wave
There is lots to be said for getting on board early with new technology. I have been immersed in the field of AR and VR since 2011 and had some interesting discussions around the merits of BIPA and the rise of the protected self in terms of data. I've been researching blockchain and working with patents owners in this area for about seven years and, although dispersed ledger technology isn't new, the use cases for it and productization of it as NFTs is on the rise. I get asked to look at use cases for blockchain projects. The rise of environmental responsibility as a basic business obligation has seen me involved in B Corp conversions and the blue economy. Because technology and business are always changing, opportunities continually present themselves to refresh your knowledge and hone in on a field of expertise that very few other lawyers may possess. As an advocate for niche, this is where I direct my efforts. Given the exponential growth in knowledge that professionals are expected to have (in general, the amount of information a worker encounters in the daily workplace doubles every 18 months),[4] it is simply not

possible to keep up with "all" of it and so specialization is a natural antidote to information overload.

Within the chosen field of specialization, it is necessary to identify those clients you know you can work with and can onboard and those you want to work with in future as your practice expands so that you have a path for development. That should not be fixed, it will need to be flexible! Use research and data tools to ascertain as much information as possible about those clients you want to pursue and target the offering of legal services to them specifically based on your collected and assessed learnings. If they have a lawyer on record, what do I do that is better, or what can I add to inform and advise on their next steps? Am I cheaper or faster and which of these is key to the client? Do I know where their industry is heading and the challenges that might arise? This way I can be proactive and not reactive (a criticism often levelled at their former lawyers by new clients).

To give myself profile, I publish, and I opine. None of this is new, it is profile and it is positioning and it is necessary in an environment where trust in human lawyers is undermined by mistakes in the profession, ever-increasing fees, nonsensical hourly rates, and the challenge that is upon us from AI lawyers and legal service providers outside of the profession.

The key to staying on board is to keep an open mind about the subject – the method of delivery may change, the technology may develop, and the clients and businesses have a cycle of growth and using technology to remain agile in that cycle and aligned to it is also key.

By opening up the door to one area, you will find you are invited to look at others. Sometimes these will be related and sometimes not, but it's the learning you take as you explore that will give you that truly niche knowledge that is so vital to creatives and innovators. Your experiences and your learnings also create trust with the clients and give you extra credibility as you have taken the trouble to immerse yourself in a subject and consider the "what ifs" and "what nexts". Once you have those, it may be the "uncommon" application of common-sense commercial principles that work best for you or your client or some little-known aspect of laws that keeps your practice relevant.

Finally, don't be shy and do put yourself forward. Ask the CTOs, the CFOs, and the CEOs if they will do this too and recommend you within their business community. Ask to speak at the founders' groups they attend, ask who they mentor, and volunteer to do all of this yourself. Personal relationships and IRL in a world full of artificial is a differentiator and a key business development skill. You never know, you might end up working with products that only exist within the black box of an AI model and you will never see, or you might end up advising a pony, a centaur, a unicorn, or even a dragon!

References

1. www.forbes.com/sites/forbescommunicationscouncil/2024/05/17/ai-is-coming-for-your-current-job/.
2. www.ipsos.com/en-us/want-understand-early-adopters-generative-ai
3. www.investopedia.com/terms/d/diffusion-of-innovations-theory.asp
4. Moore's Law and Buckminster Fuller's "Knowledge Doubling Curve", Critical Path, 1982.

Chapter 9:
Culture, connection, and collegiality – creating a model that works for female lawyers

By Sarah Goulbourne, co-founder, gunnercooke

The traditional law firm model has always promised lawyers that, should they progress to partner, they will be rewarded handsomely. The promise of ample financial compensation and the prestige of the profession remains an attractive career path for those considering their options in their late teens and early 20s.

However, the path to partner is marked with long working days and high levels of stress, often meaning lawyers have to make a decision between reaching the top or attaining an enjoyable work–life balance. Yet more recently, the current generation of NQs and associates are asking why they must choose between career success and a fulfilling personal life. The COVID-19 pandemic has only served to accelerate this feeling.

It is not surprising to find that this disproportionately impacts female legal professionals. Recent research from the Solicitors Regulation Authority indicates that while there are slightly more women (53 percent) than men working in the profession, when it comes to climbing the ladder, women account for only 37 percent of partners.[1] The law and its traditions can be resistant to change, and an enduring culture of "presenteeism" can punish women who may need greater flexibility in their careers as they start a family.

Having trodden this path myself – along with raising my own children – I knew that legal services could be delivered differently. As a general counsel, I had purchased legal services for many years and knew two things – firstly, I wanted a senior lawyer's advice as they had the experience and gravitas to support me, and secondly, I wanted to know and have confidence in the cost of the service.

I also disliked the pressure that was put upon lawyers in private practice, especially the relentless pressure to hit billable hours targets. With greater digital connectivity and smarter ways of working, there had to be a new, modern model that would be more inclusive, reduce stress, and create happier lawyers.

Experience – how being a woman shaped my career in the law

I had known that I wanted to be a lawyer since my school days. I wanted the intellectual challenge of the subject, but also to help people. It felt an exciting and interesting career choice and I'm glad I chose it.

Law is a great profession. It attracts bright, motivated people who want to help their clients and make a difference. There is intellectual stimulation, but also the chance to become a business woman too.

However, law can be slow to move with the times. I felt that in a changing world, traditional legal services were ripe for disruption. I could also see that many great female lawyers were leaving the profession when they started a family. I wanted to create a business where these women could thrive and develop their careers as they wished – help them to become business leaders building their own practice on their own terms.

Time for change – when and why I felt I could make a difference

The Legal Services Act was passed in 2010, triggering a huge amount of press coverage and speculation about how legal services could be different. This was a great time to start a new style of law firm – a firm where senior lawyers could bring their clients and work with them how, when, and where they wanted. Offering certainty of fees was core to the model too.

I had recently finished an MBA, and I drew on the many ideas and models from other sectors that I had learned about. This was integral in finessing that initial spark of an idea for the firm, shaping how we positioned ourselves from day one. We thought of ourselves as a business first that provided legal services. This meant a very different approach to traditional parts of a law firm.

Thinking back to how few senior female role models there are in the legal profession – especially female managing partners – I saw the creation of gunnercooke as setting an example that shows young female lawyers they can aim for the top. We're just one firm though – there needs to be much more positive action taken by the legal sector to stop the exodus of female lawyers in their 30s.

The reaction to our innovative model was initially mixed. Many people didn't understand what we were trying to do. The idea of lawyers being self-employed, while providing all the services they needed to operate, was very novel. However, the economic climate (just two years after the global financial crisis of 2008) meant that many talented lawyers were available to talk. Once we had pitched our vision of a firm without politics and hierarchy, where every lawyer has the freedom to design the practice they've always wanted, lawyers soon began to be interested.

My husband, close family, and friends were hugely supportive, which was very helpful in the early years. Some of my first clients were former colleagues who passed me their legal work, which gave us confidence in the viability of the model. We could test the systems and processes we were creating.

The early years – defining our mission and making it happen
Our mission and our culture are at the core of everything we do – we characterize it as our "intentional culture". From day one, my co-founder and I were focused on creating a better firm that improved the lives of everyone working there. Our mantra was, and is still, that happiness is an everyday feeling. There are three key visions that have driven gunnercooke from the start:

1. To improve the way legal and professional services are delivered to clients.
2. To help lawyers, consultants, and advisors have the freedom to design their own life.
3. To improve our communities and the lives of all those without the same opportunities we have.

These three reasons for our existence sit alongside our 13 guiding principles (behaviors that are expected of everyone who works at gunnercooke) to create the basis of the "gcWay". The is a document that introduces all who work at gunnercooke to the culture and expectations of the firm, providing guidance and support on how to contribute to the firm's shared vision.

From my perspective, I needed to make sure we were demonstrating that law could be practiced in a different, more modern way that would provide a more equitable environment for women. We explained to female lawyers interested in joining the firm that they would have the freedom to be parents and lawyers, working on their own terms. Moving away from the traditional law firm structure – no boss, no hierarchy, no politics, no targets – would keep women in the sector, still able to operate at the most senior levels, without adding undue pressure to family relationships.

Our model wasn't just for the benefit for women with children either – the gunnercooke model invites female lawyers to build their own practice in the way they want, freeing them from the constraints of gender stereotypes that still exist in many workplaces.

It is not enough of course to just write down a mission, values, and an idea of the culture we wished to create. The gcWay is critical to our success, but I knew that it could not simply exist as a dusty brochure left on a shelf, or a PDF attachment on an email that was never read. Culture has to be embedded right from the start and reinforced every day to make sure the firm stays true to itself even as it grows. It was challenging to maintain a unique culture as the success of the firm began to spread through the industry, but I was determined to keep what makes us special at the forefront of everyone's minds.

gunnercooke is founded on the importance of collegiality. This is critical when considering the model to which gunnercooke works in today's digitally-focused world. gunnercooke is not a "virtual" law firm – while its lawyers are able to work from wherever they like, the firm will succeed only if colleagues get to know each other and seek opportunities to share contacts and leads wherever possible. This provides greater work satisfaction for the lawyers, but also ensures a higher quality, seamless service for clients. So how to do this if partners are choosing to perhaps work from the office only one day a week, or exclusively remotely?

I work closely with our people and development director and her team to create a varied, innovative program of events and services that encourages lawyers to interact with colleagues whenever and however they want. A carefully designed blend of in-person and online events allows colleagues to meet, chat, and build positive relationships in a way that is most meaningful for them. Every week there is something happening that connects colleagues. There are too many to detail here, but highlights include:

- A virtual "coffee roulette" (where lawyers are matched at random with another person from anywhere in the firm) can be squeezed in the diary to facilitate an online introduction.
- Our summer walks program that allows colleagues to get together in-person, in the great outdoors, in an entirely relaxed fashion.
- Support groups led by lawyers with a particular interest in that topic. One such group has been set up for lawyers who have autistic children to share their experiences and exchange tips.

New starters are invited to welcome day events, where we make them feel like part of the family immediately. The highlight of the calendar is gunnercooke's annual symposium, where colleagues from across the world convene for three days in Oxford to hear from inspirational leaders and relax with colleagues in some of the world's most beautiful surroundings. We even have our own in-house TV program!

Connection is vital in building our happy community of lawyers. Yet a key part of the firm's culture is encouraging everyone who works here to find ways to improve not only their own lives and those of their clients, but of those in their local community. "Purpose" is a frequently overused word in corporate communications these days, but my co-founder and I wanted our firm to be one that is always outward-looking, looking for ways to pass on some of the privilege that those in our profession enjoy to those who might not have the same means or connections.

By creating a charitable foundation that sits alongside the firm, gunnercooke is able to offer its lawyers many opportunities to support their local communities. These range from traditional charity walks and fundraisers, through to more innovative concepts. gcScholar, for example, ensures that for every student who secures a placement with the firm through family connections, gunnercooke sources a student without access to those connections and provides them with a placement. To tackle that most modern scourge of loneliness, gunnercooke has opened a bricks-and-mortar bookshop in the center of Manchester, dedicated to connecting with those at risk of loneliness and isolation. Giving back with a sense of purpose is part of the DNA of the organization, showing compassion in action.

Lawyers with a clear purpose are happier lawyers, and happier lawyers mean happier clients. Happier clients – well, that's how you grow your client base and your profits.

Profit with purpose is not just possible, it's a sustainable, authentic way to grow the firm. Going back to the basics of how revenue is earned in a law firm, it's simple – you carry out more work for existing clients or you find new clients.

Expanding services to existing clients is a lot easier. The mission and culture of a law firm is essential to this. For example, at gunnercooke, our commitment to making our lawyers happier, delivering the best service to our clients, and leaving the world a better place than we found it makes us a more attractive partner for both prospective and existing clients.

New clients are harder to obtain as you have to attract them from another law firm. I mentioned earlier that a spirit of collegiality is key. When thinking about attracting and retaining clients, this culture allows a lawyer to introduce other partners and collaborate, and so it must be continually nurtured. It is also important to remember that our fee-share structure motivates lawyers to help each other win work.

We also deliberately positioned the firm as having a full-service offering, which allows us to keep more fees within the company.

Celebrating success – how women at gunnercooke have made their mark
When I started gunnercooke, there were many applications from female partners who were considering leaving the legal profession due to the seeming impossibility of a healthy work–life balance. It is due in some part to our culture and structure that there are so many successful women lawyers in gunnercooke. We have consciously created an environment in which women can reach the most senior levels without compromising their earning potential.

I'm proud to have grown this firm to over 400 partners since we started in 2010 – 40 percent of whom are female. I am proud to have been recognized myself by a number of legal and business awards for my work in creating gunnercooke, but I'm also very proud to say there are so many success stories from women across the firm.

One of our partners joined us when she had two very young children, bringing one client to the firm. Just six years later, she has built her own team of lawyers to support her and has forged relationships with two colleagues to create a combined force to populate their new business pipeline and to optimize client service.

She has over time developed an excellent personal brand in the firm, proactively executing business development plans to encourage new clients into her practice. She has also opened herself up to having a business coach, who has supported her in growing her business. I'm very proud of gunnercooke's coaching offer, which supports our partners in thinking of themselves as business people – not just lawyers.

The firm has the culture, structures, and support in place to lift women up as they reimagine their careers in the way they've always wanted. What has been extremely rewarding is seeing this supportive culture be embraced by our partners and amplified. Employment partner Rachel Spink has recently founded The Female Lawyers' Club,[2] a community for female lawyers where members can seek advice, support, and mentorship from each other, challenging barriers and talking about the issues that affect female lawyers.

It's not just in the UK that we're changing things for women in the law. Our US office is led by Noreen Weiss, featured on Super Lawyers (the list of the top US lawyers), and also an officer at the International Bar Association.

These independent endorsements demonstrate how so many of the women choosing to work at gunnercooke are truly inspiring.

This I have learned – passing on the wisdom
If I could pass on one thing I've learned to women working in law today, it is this – taking control of your own career may not be as daunting as you might think. Having a work–life balance as a legal professional in the 21st century is not an unobtainable aspiration – it is possible to design, set up, and scale the successful practice you've always wanted. If management meetings and office politics are taking up time unnecessarily, make them a thing of the past!

I consider it a privilege to be able to support women in the earlier and middle stages of their legal career. As part of their own development, female lawyers may also wish to explore mentoring of more junior lawyers to grow a team and recruit associates – it's something that gunnercooke believes in strongly and is part of our support framework.

I'd also say that isolation can be a real enemy of success. Find ways to work with others. Something I'm particularly proud of is how we've proved the power of collegiate working for our partners through our international collaborative network of lawyers.

So, what is the secret to success as an ambitious woman in today's legal industry? It's finding the right place and the right support to help you to believe in yourself. You can achieve whatever your goal is. You have succeeded already in becoming a lawyer, so now it's about working out the lawyer you want to be. Have a plan and be ambitious in defining your goals. Work with a coach or mentor, and never, ever, be afraid to ask for help.

Don't be afraid to try something, even if it doesn't work. The worst thing is not trying.

References
1   www.sra.org.uk/sra/news/press/2023-press-releases/2023-firm-diversity-data-pay-gaps/
2   https://femalelawyersclub.com/

Chapter 10:
What business development means to in-house lawyers – in conversation with top GCs

In today's rapidly evolving business landscape, the role of in-house lawyers has transcended beyond traditional legal counsel to become integral drivers of business development and strategic growth. In this chapter, we delve into the insights and experiences of three GCs, who share their perspectives on how in-house legal teams can contribute to business development. Our GCs discuss the challenges and opportunities they face, the skills required to align legal functions with business objectives, and the evolving expectations of in-house legal departments. Their insights provide a comprehensive understanding of the vital role in-house lawyers play in shaping the future of their organizations.

Aniela Foster-Turner, ENODA
Aniela is a senior executive with over two decades of international legal and compliance experience in the energy sector. Aniela is the general counsel for Enoda, a tech company in the energy sector.

What does business development mean for an in-house lawyer?
Business development is crucial for all functions, including the general counsel and legal in-house team. Although historically, the in-house lawyer was there to provide a legal opinion when requested, to analyse and research, and perform consultancy functions, this role has evolved and changed enormously during my 25+ years career. Business development encompasses a team effort of driving strategic growth, market penetration, diversification of product / services, team development, and building strategic partnerships. The in-house legal function plays a key role in each of these segments, contributing to strategic and business deliberations and adding value to the organization.

    Reputation and trust are paramount for business development, so the legal function occupies a pivotal role, protecting the organization's integrity, guiding the company during both stable and unsettled times, communicating with internal and external stakeholders, and protecting the organization while also facilitating growth.

As a GC, what does a day in your life look like?
No day is the same so there are so many things I could talk about.

I start my day with a bit of compliance and corporate governance over breakfast. A GC role navigates through a labyrinth of regulatory requirements and safeguards the company from any potential risks. So, I am always on the lookout for any overnight developments and assessing the potential impact on the team, business, and industry and finding original and innovative solutions.

The best part of the morning is spent with key stakeholders, identifying the priorities, aligning on strategy, mitigating events and incidents, briefing on various legal findings etc. If I am not negotiating contracts, or advising the business on complex transactions – I am scrutinising corporate documents, preparing board documents, looking at intellectual property, M&A, property, or litigation matters, employment, and data security issues with various colleagues in the business or corporate functions so that we identify the areas we can support. We always try and be a step ahead.

Midday is all about the team. Either grabbing a coffee and a sandwich with the team or over a one-to-one, we talk development, training, webinars, and new initiatives. We always aim to identify quicker and smarter ways of doing things so that we remain curious and innovative.

Afternoons and evenings are for more business meetings, management of external advisors, networking with peers, and volunteering. There is lots of ground to cover – commercial, corporate, industry-specific, as well as legal operations, so the bigger the challenge, the more excitement it brings.

What do you think is the most important area to focus on when refining one's business development skills?
The general counsel and in-house legal functions occupy a pivotal leadership role, so a skills toolkit that caters for decisive decision-making, strategic perspectives, and problem-solving abilities is needed. Enhancing those key strategic and leadership abilities, with an appetite for learning, upskilling, and keeping up with legal and industry developments is key. This involves a deep understanding of strategic perspectives, problem-solving abilities, ESG, and governance. Approaching legal tasks must be done through business lenses and includes commercial awareness, pragmatism, as well as sound judgement – these are essential ingredients for a successful in-house lawyer.

What can GCs and other senior in-house lawyers do to support other women at their company?
Encourage, empower, and create a platform for their development. Role modelling and facilitation of resources for training and development sessions is key to deal with some of those most frequent issues (confidence, lack of flexibility, stereotypes, micro aggressions, etc.). Mentoring, coaching, sponsorship, and network opportunities are all important tools that should be made available. Leadership programmes and educational platforms are a must.

Lastly, what do you think women private practice lawyers can learn from in-house in terms of business development?
Understanding the behind-the-door work of taking an idea on paper to a multibillion business and all the steps that are built with each part of the business team to make it happen (involving commercial, technical, and legal skills). As well as that "can do" attitude and being comfortable being uncomfortable to continually assess and examine how innovation can be deployed for the benefit of the business. Reframing challenges as opportunities, moving away from the shame and blame culture, and always prioritizing wellbeing and "one-team" approach.

The legal team must be led from a core of meaning, so driving a cultural change of sharing knowledge, optimism, and role modelling is key to ensure personal and team development and alignment with the wider vision and mission.

Hannah Constantine, Smiths Group plc
Hannah Constantine is a lawyer with wide corporate, M&A, and commercial experience. She is currently general counsel for corporate and M&A at Smiths Group plc, a FTSE 100 engineering group.

What does business development mean for an in-house lawyer?
Ultimately, business development for in-house lawyers is about creating relationships with people, whereby they value your ideas, input, and help. People will seek collaboration with people they trust and like – so business development is about showing your stakeholders that you can be trusted to help solve their difficulties and enhance their successes, no matter what the subject matter – and that working with you is fun.

For me, this has meant being generous with my time, being actively involved in what the business is doing day-to-day (not only when there is a legal issue), and being eager to learn, share, help confront difficult topics constructively, spot hidden angles, offer opinions, and make decisions. That way, when someone needs a lawyer or just a sounding board, you are easy to think of and contact.

As a GC, what does a day in your life look like?
I get up at 5.30am to exercise. This sets me up physically and mentally for the day, and I really notice the difference if I don't make time for it.

In my global role, I wake up to a lot of overnight emails from other timezones. I clear as many quick responses as I can on my train into the office and think through more complex matters.

There is a lot of variation in my role. I've always got M&A matters and disputes, new regulations to understand and communicate, and plenty of less legal matters like continuous improvement projects, resourcing, budgeting, and process design. I run three different sub-teams and make regular time to think about opportunities that can challenge my teams and let them shine. In reality, I bear my fair share of admin too.

At the end of the day, I return home to an exuberant greeting from the dog and take her for an evening walk, which provides a welcome reset. I try to reflect on what problems I've solved – I get the most satisfaction from having made someone's day easier – as well as what is still to improve. An hour on the sofa is a good opportunity to sow creative seeds. I try to check out of emails after 8.30pm unless anything is urgent and get enough rest to recharge for the next day..

What do you think is the most important area to focus on when refining one's business development skills?
It's important to focus on the success of your client's or stakeholder's business (rather than your own legal business), and to come across as a human (who just happens to be a lawyer). Take the time to consider how your clients experience your interactions.

This means doing research and asking questions to understand your stakeholder's business – its unique make-up, risks, opportunities, and pain points. And to understand your stakeholder as a person – including their previous experiences, their appetite for risk, and their potential blind spots. If you do these things, you will give bespoke and relevant advice that they value.

What can GCs and other senior in-house lawyers do to support the other women at their company?
Ask how you can most usefully support them, rather than making assumptions about what they need from you. If they're in a different part of the business from you, they might have challenges that you haven't considered.

Celebrate their successes without being asked to. And don't just tell them how impressed you are – tell their managers too.

Introduce them to people in your network so more people can see their potential and offer them different perspectives. Sometimes there's value in introducing them to people who have experiences / perspectives that contrast with their own – it's not all about commonality.

Lead by doing. Be a role model for speaking up with authenticity and respect. Show that warmth is not the enemy of gravitas and you can have both.

Lastly, what do you think women private practice lawyers can learn from in-house in terms of business development?
In the in-house environment, you come into regular contact with your stakeholders. You bump into them at the coffee machine or at meetings on a wide range of projects and build strong relationships during the good times. So, when they need help or advice, you spring to mind easily. Whereas in private practice you may have little natural contact with your clients in between live matters – and you might be one of several lawyers they could call – so you need to look for ways to have that "little and often" interaction that puts you in your client's mind and lets them get to know and trust you as a person. I've seen private practice lawyers do this successfully by sending on relevant news articles they've seen, by asking if I have 20 minutes for a coffee because they just happen to be passing my office, and by opening authentic discussions on topics that allow us to compare our values and beliefs. Low-key is better here, and listening is more important than overt selling. If you always have a product to sell, the trust is harder to build.

Misha Patel, JDG
Misha is a seasoned English law-qualified corporate / commercial lawyer and the general counsel at JDG, a leading professional services platform provider.

What does business development mean for an in-house lawyer?
Successful business development for in-house teams hinges on a multifaceted skill set that transcends traditional legal expertise. For an in-house

lawyer, this means earning the trust and respect of the entire organization. This goes beyond delivering exceptional legal work. It involves demonstrating a deep understanding of your company's core operations, industry trends, and strategic objectives. Proactively addressing and anticipating potential challenges and opportunities is crucial. Building strong relationships with stakeholders and aligning your legal counsel with business goals showcase your value in driving growth. Strategic (even if it's uncomfortable or unnatural to do!) self-marketing and providing commercially astute legal guidance are essential. Exceptional communication skills are vital, as you must articulate legal concepts clearly to non-legal stakeholders while fostering collaborative relationships across departments. It's essential to not only build and nurture strong, authentic relationships throughout the organization but also externally. Excellent project management and technological adeptness are pivotal in navigating complex projects and leveraging digital tools to enhance efficiency and productivity.

You're not just a legal advisor – you're a trusted and indispensable partner in the company's success, fostering a culture of compliance and ethical business practices. The ability to build and sustain strong relationships, balance legal rigor with entrepreneurial acumen, adaptability, and a client-centric mindset defines the skill set necessary for exemplary business development in the in-house legal arena.

As a GC, what does a day in your life look like?

My days are a whirlwind of activity, brimming with new challenges and opportunities. Each day starts with a quick scan of urgent emails to set priorities based on the company's immediate needs and ongoing projects. I dive into meetings and calls with various team members to discuss the legal implications of business decisions, navigate contract negotiations, address resource matters, and assess our client pipeline. Strategic planning sessions with the executive team are a key part of my role, aligning legal strategies with our business goals.

Throughout the day, I collaborate closely with the C-suite, manage pressing internal and client matters, review and draft a variety of contracts, and oversee litigation risks and corporate governance. Mentoring and managing our legal staff plays a significant role in my responsibilities. Balancing these diverse tasks keeps me on my toes and requires sharp time management and a deep understanding of both the legal and business landscapes. Every day is different, but that's what makes the role both exciting and fulfilling.

What do you think is the most important area to focus on when refining one's business development skills?
The heart of successful business development lies in building strong, trusted relationships – creating bonds with clients, colleagues, and industry peers that are so solid they become the cornerstone of your professional success. For in-house lawyers, this means understanding the needs and goals of different departments and finding ways to support them with your legal expertise, insight, and calm demeanor (especially when everything around you is frantic). Becoming an indispensable partner within your organization is key. Networking within the industry and keeping a pulse on market trends can unlock doors to strategic partnerships and exciting collaborations. The magic happens when you combine effective communication, genuine empathy, and an initiative-taking approach to problem-solving. These skills transform ordinary interactions into powerful connections that drive your business development efforts to new heights.

What can GCs and other senior in-house lawyers do to support the other women at their company?
Supporting other women at my company involves mentorship, advocacy, and fostering an inclusive environment. I actively mentor others, provide career guidance, share insights, and offer constructive feedback to help individuals navigate career challenges. Having personally benefited from mentorship, I understand its power in building confidence and advancing careers.

I advocate for others by ensuring their contributions are recognized and valued. This includes recommending them for high-visibility projects, promotions, and leadership roles, and speaking up on their behalf in meetings and decision-making processes. Advocacy also means promoting fair and unbiased practices in recruitment, retention, and promotion to create an equitable workplace.

I create, participate in, and support internal and external women's networks, professional development programs, and industry networks (such as the Asian Women's Network and the Eagle Club) to facilitate knowledge sharing, peer support, and a sense of community. These groups provide opportunities for women to connect, share experiences, and support each other at all levels.

Lastly, I lead by example, championing work–life balance through flexible and remote working arrangements, ensuring these policies are accessible and can be utilized without stigma.

Supporting each other in these ways creates a ripple effect, fostering a workplace culture where everyone feels respected and empowered to thrive. I absolutely love this quote:

"Always remember that leadership is a privilege. Your influence can alter the trajectory of people's careers and transform their entire lives".

Lastly, what do you think women private practice lawyers can learn from in-house in terms of business development?

The legal market has undergone significant change as firms navigate fierce competition, pricing pressures, heightened client demands, increased regulation, technological advancements, and disruptive new entrants. Business development for private practice lawyers has evolved from internal marketing teams, outsourced agencies, and dedicated client development roles. Yet, regardless of gender, the fundamentals remain – build a strong reputation through expertise, establish trust and credibility, listen actively to clients' needs, understand their business, and nurture relationships at all levels.

In-house lawyers, deeply integrated within their organizations, provide tailored legal advice aligned with corporate goals. Private practice lawyers can enhance their business development by further adapting this approach – understanding clients' business models, industry challenges, and long-term objectives.

In-house lawyers excel at building broad corporate relationships, a skill private practice lawyers can leverage to strengthen client connections, cross-sell services, and expand their networks. Adopting a proactive, business-oriented and client-centered mindset will elevate business development efforts in private practice and cement a firm's position as the in-house team's preferred external expert.

I've also been fortunate to participate in client training sessions, mentoring programs, women's networks, and senior lawyer forums hosted by both female and male private practice lawyers. These invitations, often extended regardless of whether I've engaged their services, have been instrumental in solidifying business relationships. The lawyers who maintain a natural, authentic relationship with me are at the forefront of my mind when I seek external expertise. This organic approach underscores the power of genuine connections and strategic relationship-building in business development for the long-term.

It's about expressing genuine interest in your clients and their work, understanding their business, fostering loyalty, and maintaining personal connections alongside professional focus. By cultivating authentic relationships and demonstrating a deep commitment to clients' success, private practice lawyers can significantly enhance their business development strategies.

Chapter 11:
Mentoring and coaching

By Claire Rason, Client Talk

Mentoring and coaching are experiencing a bit of boom. Everywhere you turn, someone either seems to have a coach, is a coach, or is talking about mentoring. The terms "mentoring" and "coaching" are used interchangeably, but whilst there are overlaps, the two are different and in this chapter we set out the differences between them. The chapter will help you understand which to choose and to consider how they might support you with business development.

What is the difference between mentoring and coaching?
Coaching is often thought of in terms of performance, specifically performance enhancement. This is partly because the term first became popular in sports. It is true that a significant part of coaching relates to behavioral change and helping people perform at their best. However, this does not mean remedial, which is something that people often think about when the term coaching is used inside firms. Performance enhancement also doesn't mean that coaches offer advice. In fact, a quick way to spot whether a coach has a high level of expertise is to see whether they fall into the trap of giving advice.

    A coach can be best thought of as a thinking partner. They are someone who can ask challenging questions and hold up a mirror to reframe and challenge thinking. The absence of advice-giving means that coaches do not need to have any experience of the area their coaching client ("coachee") wants to work on. They use specific tools to unlock the knowledge of the coachee themself. Many are humanistic – they believe that for individuals to grow they need an environment that provides them with unconditional positive regard. This sits with psychologist Carl Rogers' belief that, *"As no one else can know how we perceive, we are the best experts on ourselves"*.[1]

    Mentoring can also be thought of as helping people perform at their best, which is possibly where the conflation of terms stems from. Mentoring, however, is different from coaching. Advice is often given by mentors, and for this reason mentoring is often given by senior team members who impart knowledge to more junior members. Mentoring is where someone with experience of a topic or specialism provides guidance and support to someone else. Interestingly, this term often gets confused with sponsorship. Mentors can be sponsors, but they don't need to be.

Mentors are more often than not unpaid for their mentoring and are drawn from within the organization. They do not need to have formal training or accreditation. Coaching isn't a regulated industry, but top tier coaches have been trained and they are accredited. If you are thinking about getting a coach, ask what body they are accredited with and ask to see their credentials.

Good coaches sometimes draw on the experience they have and they can provide context where it serves the coachee. Good mentors also recognize that not all situations are the same and that things they have done and experienced will have worked because of the unique set of circumstances they were in.

A good mentor will draw on his or her knowledge but will not impose it on his or her mentee and, of course, not all mentoring is top down! Reverse mentoring is increasingly commonplace and incredibly powerful. This is where someone senior in the organization learns from some of his or her more junior counterparts. This can be particularly helpful for leaders who want to gain a perspective from the people they lead.

Mentoring
- Benefit from knowledge of someone who has done it before
- Mentor can also act as a sponsor in the firm
- Tends to be informal/unpaid
- Gives advice

Provides rich learning

Increases confidence

Challenges

Enhances performance

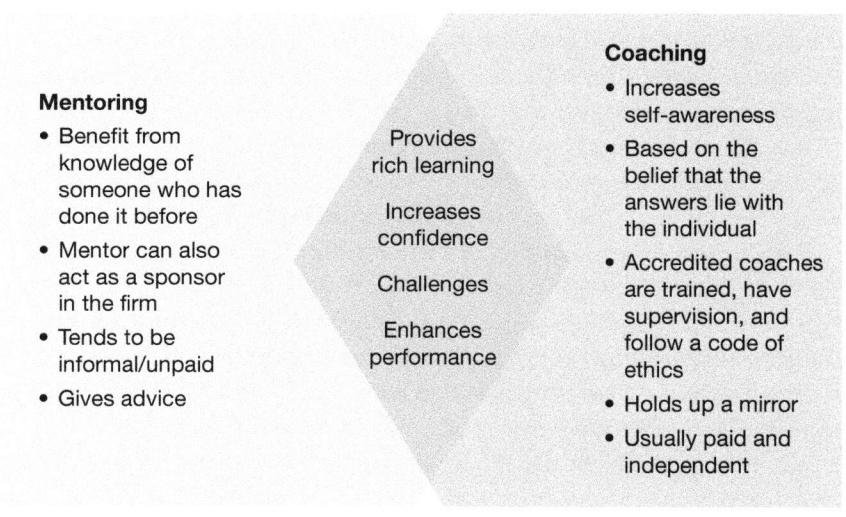

Coaching
- Increases self-awareness
- Based on the belief that the answers lie with the individual
- Accredited coaches are trained, have supervision, and follow a code of ethics
- Holds up a mirror
- Usually paid and independent

Figure 1: An example of how a coach and a mentor might differ in their approach.

Let's take a look at an example of how a coach and a mentor might differ in their approach to a particular business development challenge (see Figure 1). Let's imagine that a senior associate is looking at drawing up a business case for partnership. Part of the business case is to set out a personal business development plan. The senior associate has doubts about her ability to write a plan that she can action. She broadly knows what needs to be included, but she doesn't want to "overpromise and underdeliver".

What will happen if she fails? A coach would work with the associate to explore her thinking. They would ask questions to explore what she has done well already and help her to reframe her doubts and limiting beliefs. They would help build confidence in her ability to deliver. They would also create experiments for her to move outside of her comfort zone and to try new things. To get comfortable with failure. This might lead to her developing a more stretching personal business development plan.

A mentor in this example might be a partner in the firm, male or female. They might explain to the associate what they put in their personal business development plan. They might speak about the things that worked – and that didn't – for them. They might provide the associate with examples of where they have seen them succeed in the past, or perhaps share stories of other associates and what they did to both write and deliver a plan. A mentor might provide comments and ideas for the plan itself. This approach will dig into what the associate has written and a mentor might help to redraft it. A mentor could also help the mentee see that it doesn't matter if they fail at certain things – that's part of the process.

Both of these approaches have value, and as has been highlighted, skilled mentors and coaches might share elements of each approach. The key difference is that the coach will draw on the experiences and perceptions of the senior associate themselves. The mentor, by way of contrast, will provide examples of their own and give advice.

How coaching and mentoring are relevant to business development

The author's research (The Class of 2002)[2] has shown that one of the reasons why females opt out of partnership is because they don't feel confident in their ability to do business development. Books like this are a great way to shine a light on the fact that women can excel at business development without turning into the caricature of an alpha rainmaker. However, what sits behind the limiting belief – that many lawyers have – that "they can't do business development"?

It is not only the author's own research that has shown how a lack of confidence around business development can impact female progression. Other studies have shed light on the importance of confidence in the representation of women in senior leadership roles. A recent study[3] by Dr Susan Rose and Fiona Wilkinson examined the effect that low self-confidence has on gender balance in leadership.

In line with the Class of 2002 and other studies, Rose and Wilkinson found that female self-confidence is impacted by assumed masculine characteristics in leadership. This makes sense – why should women be confident in assuming characteristics that haven't served them to get where they are? There are parallels here with confidence in business development for female lawyers. Where women see business development as being the same as "being a rainmaker", they are likely to lack faith in their ability to adopt a style that is alien to them. Being someone you are not is hard and doomed to failure!

What makes it rain if not the rainmakers?
I like to use the analogy of rain catcher, rather than rainmaker, for those individuals able to generate substantial revenue. Business development is rarely done in isolation and it is part of a bigger process of marketing and sales. Rainmakers will have the backing of a brand, and a team of people around them (both to deliver the work and also to win the work). It is this broader collective that "makes it rain".

Thinking that the rainmaker model is the only way to do business development is faulty thinking and is problematic. Rainmakers are best thought of as the key sales people in a firm. They catch the rain. Firms need sales people; however, firms also need marketeers and business developers. They need to make it rain too!

Thinking that rainmakers are the whole sales funnel is a problem – it undervalues the importance of the team. Unless you are a sole practitioner, you are likely to be in a place where you have a range of professionals who are all good at different things. You will have a team of marketing and business development experts who are good at marketing and business development – that's what they have been hired to do.

Business development is about relationships. In large firms, there are complex webs of relationships. These are created by teams working together. Understanding what you bring to the team is key. Understanding who can fill the gaps that you can't, and being open to being vulnerable – admitting that someone else is better placed to do something – is arguably the best way to "do" business development.

The myth that one person has to be good at everything is damaging and unnecessary and – in the context of confidence in business development – means that many female lawyers don't do any for fear of failure.

Confidence and business development

Confidence is faith in our skills and capabilities. It is being sure of ourselves. Confidence is something that coaches often explore with their coachees. Many conversations start there. It is central to how motivational interviewing (a subset of coaching also used as a counselling approach) results in behavioral change. However, it is also a theme that runs across many coaching conversations and as such there are many ways coaches can tackle it.

I am a senior coach, but also a former head of marketing and business development at a large UK regional law firm. For me, it is a constant frustration that the terms "marketing" and "business development" are used interchangeably. Even business development is a phrase that seemingly covers a range of things, depending on who you talk to.

In some professional services firms, the term "business development" is a synonym for marketing. In others, it is used to cover the entire sales funnel. Then there are the firms that use business development to mean selling and some even mergers and acquisitions. It is no wonder then that the term business development can lead to confusion – and a lack of confidence. Many are not even sure they fully understand what it is.

When I talk about business development, I do so in terms of the traditional sales funnel. This model has stood the test of time, and whilst there are other models that adapt and change the funnel, such as the sales flywheel, I believe that the funnel remains the best way to understand what business development is and how it is connected to other functions inside law firms.

At the top of the funnel we find a large number of people (these could be prospects, clients, or referrers). Here we are looking to raise awareness of the firm and what it does. It is here that we employ a marketing strategy. Many firms will use a variety of tactics here and often these sit with a dedicated marketing team to deliver.

Let's take an example – writing an article for a website. This is something lawyers often have to do, often at the bequest of the marketing team. Article-writing has a myriad of benefits, but when used to raise awareness it is not business development, it is marketing.

The next stage of the funnel is where relationships start to form. Prospects or potential clients who have been made aware of the services you offer start to become more interested in what you do. It is the job of business development to nurture these clients and to move that interest to desire or consideration. That article you wrote? Perhaps you have a contact who has mentioned they are interested in the topic. You could send it to them with an invitation to speak about it face-to-face. That's an example of business development – or creating relationships.

The final stage is all about converting interest and desire into clients. This is about action – signing on the dotted line. It can be thought of as selling, and it is what many firms think of when they discuss business development. It is why firms put rainmakers on a pedestal. However, this is only one piece of the puzzle.

Furthermore, once clients have been created, the next step is to develop and nurture these relationships. This can also be thought of as business development.

Relationships take time to build and do not necessarily following a linear path. What makes a good business developer in a law firm? Someone who understands that the technical and the legal are a given. Someone who understands that it is all about people. Someone who understands relationships. All relationships are different, and that is therefore the beauty of business development – there is more than one way to succeed at it.

The constant merging of terms and noise around rainmakers means that many lawyers fear getting it wrong. It generates a lack of confidence, which then provides a barrier to giving things a go.

What is business development if not relationship management?
When I speak to firms about what they would like to achieve in the context of business development, I hear, "We want to be a trusted advisor". Some expand on this with, "We want our clients to come to us with all of their needs, we want to bypass procurement and we want to win more work".

Interestingly, if you were to ask these same people what rainmakers do, that is probably close to what they would come up with. Rainmakers achieve success in this space.

So, what is a trusted advisor? All firms want to be one and many use these words, or similar, in their marketing literature. A quick internet search reveals things such as "the firm has a seat at the client's table", or "they work collaboratively", or "they are strategic partners". Other definitions point at there being genuine emotion and say that being a trusted advisor is having a deep relationship with your clients.

The trust equation is useful here. It comes from a book called *The Trusted Advisor*[4] and it has stood the test of time. Some of the elements of the equation are hard to achieve, particularly intimacy. However, it is intimacy, combined with self-orientation, that really moves an advisor to that trusted status. And it is EQ (emotional intelligence, or emotional quotient) that will get advisors there. EQ and rainmakers are often not terms that go together (and that is not to say that they cannot).

Rainmakers are revered because they bring in work. However, clients want to have an advisor they can trust. Clients want advisors who understand them and who they are comfortable with. They want someone they can get on with.

The charismatic rainmaker is often someone who draws people in. However, other clients will be drawn in by the good listener, or the person who is a stickler for details. In other words, there is more than one way to achieve the aim. Perhaps what the rainmaker has, which others don't, is confidence.

It is at this point that we can think again about the difference between mentoring and coaching. A coach at this juncture might ask the coachee questions such as:
- What does being a relationship builder mean to you?
- What are your strengths and weaknesses when it comes to building relationships?
- How can you leverage those to strengthen the relationships that you have with clients?

A mentor at this juncture might explore and share examples of the relationships that they have with clients. They might provide some thoughts about what works and what does not. They might have a view on rainmakers and how that fits with business development within the firm. They might provide some feedback on what they have observed their mentee do well.

Both of these approaches will help the lawyer think about business development and what it means to them. Coaching will help support confidence, while mentoring might help give permission for mentees to do things their way.

What are the limiting beliefs that commonly show up around business development?

Outside of the big one – "I cannot do business development" – there are many limiting beliefs that abound here. Limiting beliefs are those internal narratives that we tell ourselves. They are the stories about ourselves that we believe to be true and that stop us from doing something.

There are two limiting beliefs that often show up in the context of business development. One appears around presentations, the other around cross-selling. There are others of course, but in sharing these two we hope to show you how coaching and mentoring can support you on your path to business development mastery, overcoming some of these traps of our own making.

Presentation skills are often seen as a key business development skill. From speaking at large conferences, through to standing up in a pitch selection meeting, there is an extent to which it is true that all lawyers need to be able to present. The problem with presenting is that it isn't just about knowing the subject matter. There are many subject matter experts that come out in a cold sweat at the thought of standing up in front of an audience. The bigger the expert, the bigger the audience, and the more likely it is that some will do anything to avoid being exposed. They are unlikely to advertise that it is nerves that are getting in the way – they can turn to a number of excuses, from being too busy, through to not seeing the value.

Many lawyers fear presenting. They know that they have to do it, but they can't think of anything worse. Fear then gets in the way when they stand up, they get bad feedback, and the experience underlines why they should never have done it in the first place.

The core limiting belief here is that "I am not any good at presenting".

Cross-selling is the holy grail of business development. It is often thought of as easy (we have all heard the rhetoric that it is easier to win business from an existing client rather than a new one). However, limiting beliefs pop up here too. Often what gets in the way of cross-selling is an internal dialogue that the professional is having.

> *"Having to cross-sell will show me up as not being any good at sales."*
> *"This is supposed to be easy, what if I fail?"*

Changing limiting beliefs and assumptions is at the heart of most coaching. Coaches will have different ways to help lawyers reframe their thinking and to adopt different mindsets. It is one of the reasons why coaching is so important in the context of business development skills building.

Mentoring is less overtly about limiting beliefs, partly because mentors tend to be appointed from within firms and their main focus is as a lawyer rather than as a mentor. (Coaches, by contrast, specialize in coaching and are trained in the discipline.) However, what good mentors can do is help to break down some of the activities that individuals fear, showing them how they have approached it – perhaps even sharing some of the internal narratives that they had.

Coaching and mentoring for results

Coaching and mentoring can both be used to help lawyers think differently about business development. Both can usefully shift the focus onto what skills individuals already have that can be leveraged to achieve results. This moves the conversation from "You need to be like this" to "How can you leverage who you are to be better at business development".

In other words, coaching and mentoring can deliver the desired results from business development, rather than dictate a fixed approach to getting there. Lawyers should be encouraged to answer two key questions when it comes to business development:

1. What do you enjoy doing?
2. What are you good at?

There is a range of skills that a professional needs in order to succeed in business development. They range from technical skills and knowledge in areas such as strategy, pitching, and creating sales pipelines – to softer human skills such as influence, trust, and listening. There is then a range of tactics that can help deliver a business development strategy – things like presenting, negotiation, and personal branding.

Lawyers will have a range of these skills already, whilst others can be nurtured and developed through training and coaching. Start with those skills that you enjoy and are good at. Learn to lean into some that you are not and don't be afraid to try and fail. Use coaching or mentoring, or both, to increase your own self-awareness and build confidence. Most importantly, be honest about the internal narratives that might be getting in your way.

References

1 www.simplypsychology.org/carl-rogers.html
2 www.clienttalk.co.uk/post/the-class-of-2002-women-in-law-the-executive-summary
3 *Philosophy of Coaching: An International Journal*, Dr Susan Rose, https://philosophyofcoaching.org/v7i1/04.pdf
4 *The Trusted Advisor*, David H. Maister, Charles H. Green, Robert M. Galford (2001).

Chapter 12:
Harnessing the true potential of neurodivergent lawyers

By Pam Loch, Loch Associates Group, and Danielle Gleicher-Bates, Neurodiversikey

Imagine a world set up as an obstacle course. A world where the moment you enter it, you are battling against the system. A world where the moment you step foot into the education system, additional obstacles are placed on your course, some of them impossible to reach or fit through. The course continues into the workplace, now requiring you to jump through misshapen hoops and invisible hurdles. Let's take a moment to imagine that.

How unjust does this seem, to not just have to overcome these obstacles and barriers but to then have to contort yourself through gaps designed for others. It's not a world we wish for, nor a world where we want our teams to find themselves. But sadly, that world exists for millions.

In recent years, the spotlight has been shone on neurodiversity, and more specifically how neuroinclusive the legal profession really is. In this chapter, we will continue to cast that light, consider what neurodiversity is, the current landscape within the legal profession, and the obstacles that neurodivergent lawyers face. We will identify how the business development framework needs to change, and the steps organizations can take to tap into this talent, harness their true potential and create neuroinclusive workplaces where neurodivergent female lawyers can thrive. A place where they are not just benefiting the bottom line but also creating more engaged and better performing teams.

Navigating neurodiversity
In the early 1990s, autistic activists were forming an online autistic rights movement,[1] influenced by the civil rights movements of other groups, such as those of the gay and disability rights communities. These activists built the foundations of what we now know as the neurodiversity paradigm/ movement.

Influenced by the social model of disability, the neurodiversity movement reframes variation in neurocognitive functioning as "difference" as opposed to "deficit". This shift brings our attention to the strengths of neurodivergent individuals and invites us to embrace this form of diversity, rather than stigmatize it as "problematic", "challenging", or in need of "cure" as the medical model encourages.

If we consider the concept itself, neurodiversity encompasses all human beings – those whose neurocognitive functioning is considered "neurotypical" and those whose neurocognitive functioning is considered "neurodivergent".

What is considered "(neuro)typical" or "(neuro)divergent" is based on prevailing social norms surrounding neurocognitive functioning, or "neuronorms". A neurodivergent person's brain will function differently to that of their neurotypical counterpart, depending on their neurotype or "brain wiring". Across the neurodivergent neurotypes, differences in executive function are common and include, for example, organization, prioritization, and time management.

Individuals' neurocognitive functioning may, for example, diverge in terms of learning and processing information, communication, and sensory processing. Social and professional norms that conflict with these differences can therefore pose additional barriers for neurodivergent people. For example, socializing according to neurotypical norms can understandably be much harder for a neurodivergent person than their neurotypical counterpart.

When we are talking about neurodivergence, this encompasses many different neurodivergent neurotypes such as Autism, ADHD, the Specific Learning Differences (dyscalculia, dysgraphia, dyslexia, dyspraxia), and Tourette's.

Before considering how common neurodivergence is, we want to look at some of the misconceptions that surround neurodiversity – misconceptions that continue to fuel the stigma and create barriers in education and employment.

- *Neurodivergent individuals are all the same.* This couldn't be further from the truth, and dangerously oversimplifies neurodivergence. There is no one-size-fits-all approach – neurodivergent individuals' needs, strengths, and challenges vary enormously, depending on the person, context, and environment, and can evolve and change across their lifespan. Debunking this myth is essential when we get to looking at what the legal profession can do to embrace and enable neurodivergent lawyers in their practice – because a singular solution will simply not work.
- *Neurodivergence is a superpower.* We've heard this narrative used

frequently, typically with very good intention – to empower. But it's important to acknowledge here that using this narrative to promote neuroinclusivity in workplaces can invalidate the struggles that a neurodivergent person experiences. It can also result in unrealistic expectations for neurodivergent employees to have abilities outside human capability, setting people up for failure.
- *Neurodivergence means less capable, less competent, or less intelligent employees.* Being neurodivergent has no impact on an individual's intelligence or capability. In fact, neurodivergent employees can attain high levels of success in the workplace and given the right support, excel in their field and chosen path, be that as entrepreneurs, engineers, or in the legal sector. Many neurodivergent individuals are able to think outside of the box, inject a high level of creativity and innovation into an organization, and offer a different, and invaluable, approach to problem solving.
- *Neurodivergence is a disorder, illness, or mental health condition.* Neurodivergence is mainly neurodevelopmental, impacting how people think, learn, socialize, and process information and the world around them. It is about neurocognitive functioning, the different ways our brains work. This does not mean there is anything "wrong" or in need of "fixing" – instead, it's about understanding, accepting, and then embracing the difference. Whilst neurodivergent individuals can be more susceptible to experiencing mental health problems, this says more about their environment than their neurotype.

Let's now consider the landscape. How common is neurodivergence? What is the prevalence of neurodivergent lawyers and how is evidence gathered and monitored to really understand the neurodivergent landscape within the legal sector to then really inform and drive change?

Despite growing interest in neurodiversity and neuroinclusion, there is limited data collected to assess how common neurodivergence is beyond the wider category of disability. It is, however, estimated that one in seven people in the UK are neurodivergent,[2] which is around 15-20 percent of our population. Lexxic, a specialist neurodiversity psychological consultancy, estimates that of the 300,000 UK legal professionals, around 48,000 will be neurodivergent.[3] That's a rather large population to alienate.

Neurodiversikey®'s April 2024 report, "Uncharted Territory",[4] explored the results of its surveys investigating neurodiversity and neuroinclusivity in

legal education, training, and practice. The report looked at neurodivergent law students and legal professionals' experiences of discrimination, reasonable adjustments, and disclosure, amongst other things. The findings are rather eye-opening:
- 37.7 percent of respondents were multiply neurodivergent.
- 51.4 percent of respondents have experienced discrimination on the basis of their neurotype(s) in the legal sector.
- A staggering 74.6 percent of respondents have not disclosed their neurotype(s) to avoid discrimination in their legal education/training.
- 76.3 percent of respondents have not requested reasonable adjustments in respect of their neurotype(s) to avoid discrimination in the legal sector.
- 42 percent of respondents have been refused reasonable adjustments in respect of their neurotype(s) in the legal sector.

Let's think through these statistics for a moment. Imagine going to work each day, knowing you have to keep the way you think, feel, and experience the world around you a secret to avoid being discriminated against by your peers. Alternatively, imagine having a frank conversation with your manager to ask for the support and assistance, to level the workplace playing field and enable you to thrive, to then have this refused.

Diversity has become a common conversation in recent decades, contributing to equal rights with regard to gender, ethnicity, religion, and sexual orientation. The tide has been turned, breaking down stigmas and preventing discrimination against employees based on their biological make-up or belief system to create inclusive workforces. However, when it comes to neurodivergence, whilst we are making headway, these survey results demonstrate that there is still much to do to create a legal sector that celebrates rather than discriminates against differences.

What are the strengths that a neurodivergent lawyer brings to the sector and how can we empower neurodivergent lawyers to play to their strengths to create firm-wide benefit? The legal sector is well known for its fast-paced, demanding culture, requiring meticulous attention to detail, creative and innovative solutions for clients, and the capacity to stay on track under pressure, often for long periods. Depending on the practice area, a lawyer may require highly specialized knowledge, or a much wider breadth of expertise. It goes without saying that communication is an essential facet of a lawyer's skillset, requiring the ability to adapt and shift quickly between audiences.

Contrary to the stereotypes, a neurodivergent lawyer, like anyone else, can excel in these areas. In fact, neurodivergent strengths often compliment the qualities desired in a lawyer. For example, ADHDers often have the ability to "hyperfocus" on something they are deeply interested in – a state where the rest of the world is blocked out, enabling a high level of attention to detail and productivity, with many ADHDers having bundles of enthusiasm. Your autistic colleague could be the person you turn to for niche in-depth knowledge on account of their special interest, or the one who picks up on a pattern or detail others miss. If it's innovative problem-solving you're after, dyslexic "big picture thinking" might be just what you need, whereas your top strategist could be dyscalculic. Going back to communication, dyspraxic individuals often demonstrate strong listening and verbal skills, whereas dysgraphia is commonly associated with a good memory for detail. Neurodivergent lawyers may have valuable skill sets that a firm cannot afford to ignore.

As responsible organizations, we must always ensure that we protect and look after all our employees during their working life. Neurodivergent people can be more prone to burnout, which is only exacerbated by unrealistic expectations such as requiring an individual to be able to hyperfocus all day, every day. Like with all other candidates, if businesses wish to benefit from individuals' strengths, they must do so responsibly and commit to accommodating and supporting the "whole" employee.

So why is there a gap between neurodivergent ability and the legal sector's recognition of it? And how can we close this gap to harness this potential?

Evaluating the educational system

Let's start with the building blocks. The education system is the first barrier to legal practice that a neurodivergent aspiring lawyer faces. In a perfect society, education would be universally inclusive irrespective of neurotype – catering to differences and embracing them. Sadly, this is typically not the case. Modes and methods of teaching and assessment have remained relatively unchanged over the years, with the needs of neurodivergent learners usually accommodated as an afterthought, if at all, through reasonable adjustments.

Prevailing misconceptions, stereotypes, and stigma held in respect of neurodivergence strengthen the barriers, with the potential to hinder neurodivergent individuals' entry into, and success in, higher education. The Office for Students reports that disabled undergraduates, including neurodivergent students, have lower degree results and lower employment rates after they have completed their degree.[5] What is fueling this outcome, and how can universities really embrace this cohort to enable them to lead a fulfilling and rewarding career within the legal profession?

A university that adopts certain test or interview recruitment processes, with no flexibility, can hinder a neurodivergent student's performance, from causing emotional or sensory overload, to requiring neurotypical demonstrations of body language and communication. Such entry steps can act as automatic filters, inadvertently weeding out candidates on account of being neurodivergent.

The hurdles don't stop once a neurodivergent student has got into university. Seminars and lectures can present new challenges that individuals may not have encountered in school. The lecture hall environment can be particularly challenging in terms of auditory processing, managing distractions, and sensory sensitivity. The combination of the fast-paced nature of university, the often highly emotionally charged atmosphere, and a physical environment that for many feels like an assault to the senses, can act as an impenetrable wall before even getting to the act of learning.

If you are neurodivergent, it is likely that you have relied, subconsciously or consciously, on masking to "fit in", to cope and survive in a system that is built on neurotypicality. Stigma and discrimination reinforce the need to mask, encouraging silence and non-disclosure, forcing many students to try to manage without reasonable adjustments, putting them at a disadvantage, or even to drop out. Never mind the educational implications of masking – research shows[6] that masking is detrimental to an individual's mental health and wellbeing, creating yet another hurdle for a neurodivergent individual to navigate.

So, what is the educational solution? Let's think back to that gap reported by the Office of Students, in contrast to the the statistic the University of Hertfordshire stated that 86 percent of disabled law students earned a good degree.[7] What is happening within that institution that is enabling these students to perform? What practices are being put into play that are empowering these students and driving them forward to succeed?

Firstly, applicants are assessed on a case-by-case basis – there is no one-size-fits-all approach here. The University considers the individual (and let's note the importance of the individual) application – considering the personal, professional, and educational understanding of that case. A Study Needs Agreement (SNA) is drawn up between the University and the student to understand their learning requirements and make adjustments to their journey to ensure they can thrive within the system. These adjustments are highly individualized and wide-ranging, and can mean receiving lecture notes in advance, adjustments to the physical environment, specialist mentoring, software, adjustments to exams, flexibility with policies, and considerations in group learning classes.

This flexible, individual and tailored approach to learning means neurodivergent law students are empowered to succeed in education, and positively impact their future employment. These simple adjustments should be the reality for all neurodivergent students, not just the select few that have found a progressive university that has understood and embraced their differences.

Orientating the obstacles

Let's move on to consider some of the sticking points for a neurodivergent lawyer when it comes to progressing into legal practice. Often the coping strategies that have been developed in education are stripped away when it comes to the corporate workplace environment. A certain rigidity can follow – deadlines are shorter and less flexible, the working environment is typically not within an individual's control, and workloads can be unpredictable but must still be managed. Legal practice comes with new challenges and goals, for example, marketing yourself, navigating a plethora of spoken and unspoken professional rules, and restricted career progression routes that may not be desirable to a neurodivergent employee.

It kickstarts with the recruitment and selection process. The job description – frequently an over-complicated (yet frustratingly vague) person specification, peppered with meaningless buzzwords, or requirements of neurotypicality rather than the role in question – can result in a neurodivergent candidate self-rejecting by not applying, if they do not believe they meet 100 percent of the criteria.

During the assessment and interview process, the reliance on neuronormative notions of professionalism disadvantage and discriminate against neurodivergent candidates. This is particularly problematic with, for example, psychometric testing and automated video interviewing, which typically assesses neurotypical ways of thinking and communicating. Differences in interpreting or responding to social cues, eye contact, body language, and non-verbal communication can then be misconstrued by the interviewer as unsuitability or inability.

Historically, these alleged communication deficits have been misattributed to the neurodivergent person, whereas a growing body of evidence and theory instead suggests it is a cross-neurotype breakdown of reciprocity and mutual understanding, between the neurodivergent employee and the neurotypical peer. Surely, it's time that we started to take neurodivergent ways of thinking, communicating, and being into consideration when we are recruiting talent so that we don't lose the very thing we are looking for?

Regardless of sector or role, most people will experience nerves, apprehension, and feel the pressure to perform in advance of a formal interview. However, these feelings can be intensified if an individual experiences Rejection Sensitive Dysphoria or differences in emotional regulation, and this can then be unnecessarily exacerbated by neuroexclusive practices such as refusing to provide interview questions in advance and setting the entire process up to be a series of "surprises".

Traditional aptitude and cognitive assessments, often a tool used by employers to predict job performance, can not only induce higher levels of stress but inadvertently filter out potential talent. The evidence is beginning to grow, demonstrating that neurodivergent communication is not flawed or deficient, and that communication breakdowns are a mutual difficulty between neurotypical/neurodivergent people.

The entire recruitment and selection process, from the initial job description and advert right through to employee onboarding, needs to be thoroughly considered. All bias needs to be removed and the process made accessible to all, in order to ensure a role is filled by the best candidate, based on an assessment of their ability rather than an arbitrary, often accidental, assessment of their neurotype.

What else can become a stumbling block in the workplace?

Businesses are built on people, the interactions between them, and relationships with one another. When a neurodiverse team lacks shared understanding and does not accommodate both neurotypical and neurodivergent communication needs, we can face a mutual communication breakdown and a misunderstanding from both sides.

A neurodivergent employee who provides feedback or contributes to a discussion in an honest and direct manner can often be misunderstood as being rude. Conversely, the stereotypical "British" way sometimes takes a sugar-coating approach to feedback and can be interpreted as vague and indirect for the neurodivergent employee. If time is not dedicated to ensuring all team members' communication needs are considered and accommodated, this dynamic can create reciprocal misunderstanding.

Creating strong, performing, and progressive teams relies on mutual understandings, a genuine desire to enable all differences to thrive, and recognizing that both the neurodivergent and neurotypical employee add incredible business value. If the average employee spends a third of their life at work, imagine the impact when that workplace is structured in a way that conflicts with their needs.

Whilst every neurodivergent person is different – with their strengths, challenges, and differences – there are some commonalities that can be considered across neurotypes. These include environment, policies, and practices. The physical environment can have a huge impact on the working day. Sensory considerations such as lighting, noise, ventilation, temperature, layout, and even smells can usually be easily adjusted or worked around to accommodate individual needs, for example, noise-cancelling headphones, dimmable lighting, quiet spaces, and clearly signposted and laid out offices. As for policies and processes, flexibility is key, as is assuming competence, preserving autonomy, and having respect for neurodivergent differences.

It's vital to understand that these differences are not "fussiness" or "being difficult", but a result of different brain structures. For example, sensory overload can occur because a person's brain takes in more information than average, which can be distressing and even painful. Likewise, skills that come under executive function can be more challenging for neurodivergent people, not out of lack of effort, but because their brain is structured to be better at other things. This is where flexibility and support can be especially helpful, playing to an individual's strengths whilst putting support in place. Without adaptations, the challenges will inevitably take a toll on individuals, which could eventually lead to a talented employee reaching burnout and even exiting the organization.

Neurodiversity policies can play an important part in neuroinclusion, setting out expectations for neuroinclusivity, as well as mandating neurodiversity training to increase understanding and acceptance across the entire organization.

Finally, we wanted to consider the career progression and development of a neurodivergent lawyer within the sector and what may hinder them. As discussed in chapter two, networking is a core element of business development throughout a lawyer's career.

Whilst some neurodivergent lawyers may thrive in a niche panel discussion, others may be better suited to content creation for insight articles, or even online participation. The traditional career trajectory needs to be challenged to ensure that it encourages and enables different approaches to progression and industry recognition, without adopting a one-size-fits-all career development route. In the same vein, now is the time to challenge these traditional routes, which are not always desirable for neurodivergent lawyers, and consider alternatives such as lateral progression, enabling individuals to progress and have fulfilling careers without compromising their own needs.

Making work, work
The research, first-hand accounts, and evidence shine a light on the obstacles that a neurodivergent lawyer can face on a daily basis. Neurodiversikey®'s report, "Uncharted Territory", showcases the pervasive stigma, discrimination, and disadvantage neurodivergent people in the sector come up against to a worrying degree.

Whilst the movement to create neuroinclusive organizations is gaining momentum and traction within the sector, there is still a mountain to climb to ensure all employees are valued, and that competence and difference are not confused.

So how can an organization make work, work? What are the progressive steps that a firm can take to ensure all employees, regardless of their differences, can perform and flourish in their role?

It all begins with education and awareness raising. We need to recognize and understand the neurodivergent journey, the challenges that are faced, and the benefits that people can bring to the business table. This deep knowledge will help to break down the stigma wall, brick by brick. It will help us understand where we can make business improvements and adjustments and how we bring about internal change to truly and genuinely embrace neurodivergent employees.

Appoint a champion within the firm whose role is to spearhead that education, to craft and roll out a firmwide education program that will help create an inclusive community. Importantly, whilst no decision that affects neurodivergent individuals should be made without neurodivergent input, this champion can be a neurotypical employee who is passionate about diversity and equality. Equally, visible role models are an important part of neuroinclusivity – neurodivergent lawyers of all branches and levels of seniority who share their experiences help to raise awareness and dismantle stigma, stereotypes, and misconceptions. They can also inspire and reassure other neurodivergent individuals navigating a similar obstacle course. Surely a workforce that accepts and celebrates differences, regardless of what these are, is the workforce of the future?

Onboarding a neurodivergent lawyer needs to be a tailored, individual experience. From an office design perspective, the traditional workplace is not set up for individuals who can be overwhelmed or impacted by noise, lighting, smells, and temperature. Providing reasonable adjustments, as touched on earlier in this chapter, can enable that individual to thrive and contribute to creating an inclusive culture where every employee belongs.

And then it comes down to a sincere commitment to flexibility. How can the organization really provide a flexible working approach? If we consider, for a moment, that a neurodivergent person may work best at specific times because of differences in sleep patterns and circadian rhythms, how and why would we expect them to work "standard" business hours? Surely, if the ambition is setting them up to succeed and to provide the best service possible to clients, allowing employees to work at times and locations that suit their needs can only result in higher productivity and employee satisfaction and wellbeing?

Another interesting, and thought-provoking, point to be made here is around caring responsibilities. Not only is there high co-occurrence between neurotypes, but neurodivergence is highly heritable, meaning a neurodivergent lawyer may not only be multiply neurodivergent but may also have caring responsibilities for a neurodivergent child. An organization needs to be flexible in its approach to enabling employees with such responsibilities to manage their dependents' schooling, appointments, and care, which given the widespread problems with SEND provision, is not getting any easier to juggle.

The slight elephant in the room is the question of disclosure. The stigma and discrimination that neurodivergent people are subjected to is so prevalent, especially within the legal profession, that individuals often feel they are better off foregoing the adjustments they need and are entitled to in order to level the playing field, rather than disclosing their neurodivergence and risking discrimination. Maybe one of the most salient points here, is that this warranted reluctance to disclose means, for many people, an employer is not aware of their neurodivergence until it becomes relevant to a performance management issue, by which point the damage to the employee and their future career has already taken place.

Business development for neurodivergent lawyers
So, with all this in mind, if you are a neurodivergent lawyer, what measures can you take to raise your profile within the sector, harness the power of business development, and progress in your career?

- *Understanding you.* The starting point has to be with internal reflection – taking a look at yourself to truly understand and familiarize yourself with your own needs, strengths, and challenges. Recording achievements, and how your neurotype has contributed to your success, will not only enhance and promote your own self-esteem and confidence but will showcase the benefits that a neurodivergent lawyer can bring to the industry.
- *Neurodivergence as a USP.* Naturally, being neurodivergent differentiates you from the neurotypical majority. You can leverage this not only by highlighting your neurodivergent strengths and the different perspective you bring, but also your ability to better serve neurodivergent clients, whether that is through shared communication styles, or being able to relate to and understand your client on a deeper level, enhancing trust, and creating stronger relationships.

  This is especially pertinent in practice areas in which neurodivergent clients are overrepresented. You may even be able to utilize your position as a neurodivergent lawyer by identifying and addressing potential barriers to neurodivergent clients, making you an asset to both firms and clients.
- *Tailoring business development to your needs.* The explosive and evolving nature of social media presents a real opportunity for neurodivergent lawyers to drive their own personal brand in ways that complement and capitalize on their particular communication strengths. Creating thought-leading articles, vlogs, podcasts, or even YouTube channels on a specialist practice area or topic is a powerful storytelling tool that can foster professional development by connecting you with a broader potential audience.

  The pandemic saw a huge shift in networking – creating a world where virtual attendance is not just accepted but encouraged, to accommodate a variety of scenarios and life dispositions. Harnessing the opportunity in remote networking can be an effective way of making contacts and building your profile within your field or practice area whilst honoring your own needs and commitments. To get the best out of these platforms, be selective according to your own needs.

Whether you fare better at face-to-face or remote events, in one-on-one or group settings, the key is to work to your strengths and craft your own course, if that course doesn't already exist.
- *Career progression.* Make use of available support, be they mentoring schemes, career development workshops, or internal and external neurodiversity networks. Learning from other neurodivergent lawyers can be a source of information and guidance to help navigate your career progression path. If traditional progression is not for you, consider alternative routes such as becoming more specialized (whether that is in terms of practice area or specific tasks / processes), or even becoming your firm's go-to on neurodiversity, given its increasing commercial relevance.
- *The intersection of being a woman and neurodivergent within the legal sector.* How do neurodivergent women really move forward and progress within a profession that is male dominated and neuronormative? Female lawyers already face a glass ceiling, but when neurodivergence is added to the mix, that glass is tempered, a seemingly indestructible ceiling that can stymy progression and perpetuate self-cancellation.

Prioritizing your wellbeing is a paramount part of the strategy to shatter this barrier, and a non-negotiable component of a neurodivergent lawyer's ability to thrive in their role. This does not always come easily for neurodivergent women, who have been socially conditioned to overcompensate for both their gender and neurotype, compounded by missed, late, and mis-diagnosis. Late diagnosis is commonplace, sometimes not happening until late into a career, making the practical and emotional adjustments particularly difficult with lawyers having to relearn how to do their job in a way that is more accommodating of their neurotype.

Just as a neurotypical career will look different through its female life cycle, considering perimenopause, menopause, and maternity stages, a neurodivergent lawyer's needs, strengths, and challenges can also be impacted by these life transitions. As a result, their business development and career strategy will need to be reassessed regularly and adjusted accordingly.

Conclusion

Creating a neuroinclusive environment is not a tick-box HR exercise – it's a full business commitment and approach that is championed from the very top and felt at all levels of an organization.

Progression within the sector relies on senior support, creating neurodivergent visibility, awareness, acceptance, and ultimately changing the sector to be fully inclusive. Embracing all our differences will not just lead to a more engaged, loyal, and focused workforce but could drive competitive advantage, setting an organization apart from its peers.

Recognizing and understanding obstacles is key to the future development of female neurodivergent lawyers in the legal sector. As an industry, we need to acknowledge the need to change, to adapt, and to be open to approaching work differently. It is only then that we will slowly move to a society where neurodivergence isn't a hidden secret, but actually becomes an openly embraced element of a diverse and powerful team – one that will become more attractive to clients who have equally diverse needs.

Research has shown[8] that diverse organizations are more innovative, creative, and progressive workplaces. Is it not time then for the legal profession to really embrace a cohort of people who can excel in creative and lateral thinking, who are adept at problem solving, and who have highly analytical and logical minds?

Our lasting thought is that we need to turn the tide. Raising awareness is no longer enough – we need to take action in understanding and education. We need to level up and dismantle the ubiquitous discrimination and stigma that neurodivergent lawyers contend with. We need to create cultures where masking isn't necessary, where it is safe to unmask, where open and transparent conversations are embraced, and neurodivergent talent is recognized, welcomed, and accepted. We need a neuroinclusive movement where we appreciate and celebrate that we all, whatever our brain wiring, bring something to the table and deserve to have a seat.

After all, "great minds don't think alike".

References
1. Leadbitter K., Buckle K.L., Ellis C. and Dekker M. (2021), Autistic Self-Advocacy and the Neurodiversity Movement: Implications for Autism Early Intervention Research and Practice. *Front. Psychol.* 12:635690. doi: 10.3389/fpsyg.2021.635690
2. https://lexxic.com/resources/neurodiversity
3. https://lexxic.com/blog/how-the-legal-industry-can-embrace-neurodiversity
4. https://neurodiversikey.com/surveys
5. www.officeforstudents.org.uk/media/3828/beyond-the-bare-minimum-are-universities-and-colleges-doing-enough-for-disabled-students.pdf
6. Chapman, L., Rose, K., Hull, L., & Mandy, W. (2022). "I want to fit in... but I don't want to change myself fundamentally": A qualitative exploration of the relationship

between masking and mental health for autistic teenagers. *Research in Autism Spectrum Disorders*, 99(102), 069. https://doi.org/10.1016/j.rasd.2022.102069

7 https://barristermagazine.com/disability-is-not-a-barrier-to-success-supporting-neurodiversity-in-law-at-the-university-of-hertfordshire/

8 www.forbes.com/sites/forbesinsights/2020/01/15/diversity-confirmed-to-boost-innovation-and-financial-results/

About Globe Law and Business

Globe Law and Business was established in 2005. From the very beginning, we set out to create legal books that are sufficiently high level to be of real use to the experienced professional, yet still accessible and easy to navigate. Most of our authors are drawn from Magic Circle and other top commercial firms, both in the United Kingdom and internationally.

Our titles are carefully produced, with the utmost attention paid to editorial, design and production processes. We hope this results in high-quality publications that are easy to read and a pleasure to own.

In 2021, we were very pleased to announce the start of a new chapter for Globe Law and Business following the acquisition of law books under the imprint Ark Publishing. Our law firm management list is now significantly expanded with many well-known and loved Ark Publishing titles.

We are also pleased to announce the launch of our online content platform, Globe Law Online, which allows for easy access across firms. Details of all titles included can be found at www.globelawonline.com. Email glo@globelawandbusiness.com for further details and to arrange a free trial for you or your firm.

We'd very much like to hear from you with your thoughts and ideas for improving what we offer. Please do feel free to email me on sian@globelawandbusiness.com. Happy reading and thank you for your time.

Sian O'Neill
Managing director
Globe Law and Business
www.globelawandbusiness.com

Milton Keynes UK
Ingram Content Group UK Ltd.
UKHW050143270824
447354UK00002B/10